New Consumer Marketing

New Consumer Marketing

Managing a Living Demand System

Susan Baker

with
Margrit Bass

WILEY

Copyright © 2003   John Wiley & Sons Ltd, The Atrium, Southern Gate, Chichester,
West Sussex PO19 8SQ, England

Telephone   (+44) 1243 779777

Email (for orders and customer service enquiries): cs-books@wiley.co.uk
Visit our Home Page on www.wileyeurope.com or www.wiley.com

Reprinted with corrections November 2003, March 2004

This publication is designed to provide accurate and authoritative information in regard to the subject
matter covered. It is sold on the understanding that the Publisher is not engaged in rendering
professional services. If professional advice or other expert assistance is required, the services of a
competent professional should be sought.

Other Wiley Editorial Offices

John Wiley & Sons Inc., 111 River Street, Hoboken, NJ 07030, USA

Jossey-Bass, 989 Market Street, San Francisco, CA 94103-1741, USA

Wiley-VCH Verlag GmbH, Boschstr. 12, D-69469 Weinheim, Germany

John Wiley & Sons Australia Ltd, 33 Park Road, Milton, Queensland 4064, Australia

John Wiley & Sons (Asia) Pte Ltd, 2 Clementi Loop #02-01, Jin Xing Distripark, Singapore 129809

John Wiley & Sons Canada Ltd, 22 Worcester Road, Etobicoke, Ontario, Canada M9W 1L1

Wiley also publishes its books in a variety of electronic formats. Some content that appears in print may
not be available in electronic books.

Library of Congress Cataloging-in-Publication Data

Baker, Susan.
    New consumer marketing: managing a living demand system/by Susan Baker.
        p. cm.
Includes bibliographical references and index.
    ISBN 0-470-84482-5 (cloth: alk. paper)
1. Marketing.   I. Title.
    HF5415.B279 2003
    658.8—dc21   2003007455

British Library Cataloguing in Publication Data

A catalogue record for this book is available from the British Library

ISBN 0-470-84482-5

Typeset in 12/14 Garamond by Footnote Graphics Ltd., Warminster, Wiltshire
Printed and bound in Great Britain by TJ International, Ltd, Padstow, Cornwall
This book is printed on acid-free paper responsibly manufactured from sustainable forestry
in which at least two trees are planted for each one used for paper production.

Contents

Foreword

Samuel Curtis Johnson first built his reputation as a maker of parquet floors and then became better known for creating a new way to care for them. His legacy was a company with a small portfolio of wax-based products which evolved into the global concern that SC Johnson is today, with its global household name brands such as Pledge, Glade and Mr Muscle.

One of the basic principles that has guided the successful development of the company since its founding over a hundred years ago has been the belief that we must earn the enduring goodwill of consumers and users of our products and services.

Consumers make up one of five key groups of people to whom we believe we are responsible and whose trust we have to earn (the others being: employees; the general public; neighbours and hosts in the countries and communities where we conduct business; and the world community). In particular, we are committed to providing useful products and services throughout the world by:

- Monitoring the changing wants and needs of consumers and users;
- Maintaining close and effective business relationships with the trade to ensure that our products and services are readily available to consumers and users;
- Continuing our research and development commitment to provide a strong technical base for innovative and superior products and services.

With our strong corporate emphasis on understanding consumers and providing them with what they want, I found this book enormously appealing because it offers a very clear summary of today's context for consumer marketing and identifies the real challenges facing those of us seeking to expand markets, market share and profits.

Susan depicts for us the tectonic shift that has taken place in the economy, describing this as a move from production-driven to consumption-led. In doing so she raises relevant questions about how marketing needs to undergo a consequent shift. Most of the marketing frameworks we're all too familiar with emerged in the production-driven era and we have to ask how relevant they are in this age of the 'new consumer'. This is a consumer who is active, confident and knowledgeable, one who looks for brand experiences and whose life is being transformed by developments in IT.

The marketplace before us is no longer static and homogenous, and Susan links neatly into business trends that are being played out here. She offers a framework for organising marketing to deliver the value that consumers are looking for. In doing so, she draws on thinking from the emerging discipline of complexity science.

This is a timely and relevant book. Its stimulating content makes absorbing reading for both practitioners and scholars. I'm delighted to be continuing an SC Johnson tradition of championing consumer marketing in robustly endorsing this thought-provoking work.

Steven P. Stanbrook
President–Asia Pacific
SC Johnson

Acknowledgements

'Why have you got so many books in here?' asked my son Mark, then aged five and a half years, on entering my study at home one day. 'Because I'm writing a book' I replied. 'Why do you need so many books to write a book?' he asked.

It was a good question and I went on to explain that it wasn't just the books I needed as reference material but copies of academic papers, notes of meetings with leading practitioners, conference presentations, seminar notes, copies of student projects and dissertations, and so on and so forth. For the fact of the matter is that this book has emerged out of my years as both a practitioner and an academic, and a debt of gratitude is due to the eclectic group that has contributed to my thinking. Working at Cranfield School of Management has been a particular source of inspiration and many of my colleagues will find themselves quoted for good reason. My work in establishing the New Marketing Research Group at the School (visit www.new-marketing.org) has helped in pulling many of my ideas together. I'm grateful to Professor Malcolm McDonald for supporting me in this venture and to Dr Louise Humphries and Debbie Roberts for helping me make the Group happen.

In making this book a reality I'd like to acknowledge the patience of Claire Plimmer and her team at Wiley; the secretarial assistance from Hayley Tedder at Cranfield; the creative effort on the graphics from Joanna English; and the help given by Marion Cooper with several of the case studies. Margrit Bass, who edited this as I wrote it, was always encouraging and the book has benefited enormously from her input.

Finally, I would like to dedicate this book to the three most important people in my life – my husband Chris and our sons, James and Mark. Thank you for living this book with me.

My concluding words are again attributed to Mark. He came into my study again a week or so ago and asked why the can of polish was sitting on the floor. 'Because now the book's finished, I'm clearing up' I replied. He looked about and then said disdainfully, 'Well you haven't finished yet have you'. Proving there's nothing like children to keep your feet on the ground.

Susan Baker
May 2003

About the Author

Dr Susan Baker

At Cranfield School of Management, where she is a full time member of faculty, Susan specializes in consumer marketing, in particular understanding consumer markets, branding and international marketing. She founded and directs the New Marketing Research Group, which works together with a consortium of client organizations to understand the impact on marketing of the New Consumer (www.new-marketing.org).

A frequent keynote speaker at conferences and seminars, Susan teaches on the MBA programme and works on a variety of management development programmes for companies across all sectors – consumer, business-to-business and professional services.

Prior to Cranfield, Susan pursued a ten-year career in services marketing in leisure retailing, from which she gained senior management experience on both client and agency sides of the business, in the UK and overseas.

Outside Cranfield, she was a trustee of Consumers' Association for many years and has more recently become a trustee of Beating Bowel Cancer.

She can be contacted at s.l.baker@cranfield.ac.uk

Introduction

As a member of faculty at Cranfield School of Management I have met many senior marketers over recent years who have become frustrated that 'marketing doesn't seem to be working any more'. Companies are finding it harder to connect with consumers. CRM systems that promised so much have delivered so little. The conventional tools and techniques of marketing no longer appear to be relevant. Added to all of this, marketing's contribution to a business is constantly under question. In effect, the certainties of the marketing environment have been replaced with the uncertainties of a dynamically complex marketplace.

So, what has changed?

The answer is, a lot. The ground beneath our feet feels shaky because we are experiencing the after effects of an 'earthquake'. Almost imperceptibly, the economic plates are shifting, sending tremors through the players (brand owners and retailers on the one side and consumers on the other), rearranging a landscape that had appeared static and immovable for so long. Equilibrium is being replaced with a state of continual change and uncertainty. In a variety of small ways, the fault lines are emerging with sudden clarity. We are moving from a production-driven to a consumption-led economy, where the nature of the exchange is different, and this difference is exacerbated by the force of the internet and e-commerce. This shift is creating a number of key challenges for consumer marketing.

These challenges can be summarized as the need to:

- embrace the New Consumer;
- address the concerns of brand owners and retailers;
- help organizations develop real consumer responsiveness;
- lift marketing out of its crisis.

Companies are confronted with a new kind of consumer, one that has variously been described as 'active', 'knowledgeable' and 'postmodern'. In essence, this is a New Consumer, a creature distinctly different and identifiable from its predecessors. For this New Consumer time is a precious commodity in lives that are becoming increasingly complex. In their purchasing behaviour, New Consumers now look for brand 'experiences' over and above bundles of features and benefits. They are more marketing literate than ever before, and IT enabled. New Consumers inhabit an interactive marketplace characterized by high levels of heterogeneity, which disputes the assumptions of conventional marketing thinking.

Faced with this new marketplace, brand owners and retailers are looking to enrich and expand the strategic options open to them. The growth of retailer power is of particular concern to brand owners, who have been feeling the threat posed by industry consolidation. Further stress in the relationship stems from the continuing downward pressure on price. And adding to this is the force of globalization and debate about the viability of manufacturing. Above all, there is an imperative to balance cost reduction and sales growth.

Retailers are themselves facing daunting challenges, and first and foremost among these is a long-term pattern of declining spend. Over the past ten years the retail sector has come to represent less than half the percentage of GDP it used to command. This trend varies across sectors, forcing retailers to shift their strategies to remain profitable. Other challenges have arisen in respect to the difficulties associated with acquiring a business location and consumer expectations of price.

The aim for both brand owners and retailers is to develop greater consumer responsiveness. This means focusing on the demand side of their businesses, doing the same thing better or doing something new. To achieve this, organizations need to connect better with consumers; they need to get close enough to consumers to understand how to deliver the value that consumers are seeking in a continually adaptive and innovative way. Organizations need to learn how to work in the consumer's 'space'.

Finally, criticism about the lack of clarity surrounding marketing's contribution to a business has been a feature of reports and articles over recent years. This is, in part, driven by the difficulties surrounding the measurement of marketing effectiveness but also by the fact that marketing is both equated with business unit strategy and located within the marketing mix. Without a clear emphasis as to its role, marketing languishes in a 'no man's land' and is badly placed to provide strategic leadership.

MEETING THE CHALLENGES

Meeting these challenges head on requires a different way of conceptualizing the marketing process and a different approach to implementation. This book proposes the adoption of a value-centric approach to marketing and connecting with the new science of complexity to enable business to find a way of surviving in the face of continual change.

As the practice of marketing has evolved in response to market conditions, the underlying philosophy of a business in relation to the customers it serves has shifted. Transaction marketing was based on a sales orientation with the aim of acquiring as many new customers as possible. Profit was generated through increased sales volume. Relationship Marketing then switched the emphasis to developing greater profitability through customer satisfaction, underpinned by a retention orientation. The realities of the consumption-led economy demand that the focus of a business shifts again to consumer responsiveness, based on superior processes of insight, innovation and agility, to achieve profitability. This means replacing the focus on customer retention with a value-centric orientation.

A value-centric orientation means delivering the value consumers want to buy into and the organization wants to deliver: that is, *value on the consumer's terms*, as demanded and maybe even dictated by them. This value component marks the process of exchange that takes place between the consumer and the organization; it is the 'thing' that consumers get in return for what they give. It means moving beyond a relationship emphasis to one that has at its core the definition, creation and delivery of value. If an organization can meet the value expectations of the consumer, then a long-term and profitable relationship is more likely to follow. The key is having value as the starting point; otherwise the relationship development strategy (and the CRM tools perhaps used to deliver it) will not work as intended.

This, however, is not sufficient on its own to make marketing more effective. Organizations need to reconceptualize the marketing process to take account of the dynamically complex new marketplace. Business needs to learn how to understand complexity and find ways of responding dynamically to change. This is where marketing connects with the new science of complexity. The appeal of this to business theorists is that it provides a way of thinking about how the underlying processes and relationships in a company can be organized to survive in the face of continual change.

New Consumer Marketing emerges at the confluence of these two streams of thinking – the evolving discipline of marketing and the science of complexity. New Consumer Marketing is, therefore, different from the prevailing marketing paradigm. It is a business discipline that enables the organization to master the increasingly dynamic and complex process of going to market in a systemic and holistic way. It provides managers with a means of identifying and mobilizing people and processes to help them become as adaptive and creative as possible against the background of a complex marketing environment.

The New Consumer Marketing model is presented in Figure 0.1 and it shows quite clearly how consumer marketing can be conceptualized as consisting of the three key processes, underpinned by a value-centric orientation. The model is organic in nature, reflected in the use of honeycomb-shaped cells, each of which has a nucleus. The model encourages the synergy of emphasizing both 'people' and 'process', enabling organizations to break out of the binary thinking that has long constrained management theory. In short, the static marketing function of the production-driven economy becomes a living demand system in the consumption-led economy, leaving behind the mechanistic approaches of the former era.

The first cell in the demand system is concerned with the process of value definition; that is, the process of generating and identifying insight in order to describe and demonstrate value. This covers both traditional and non-traditional ways of generating insight, and the process of turning that insight into something actionable through segmentation.

The next cell is concerned with the process of value creation. Innovation forms the nucleus of this cell and is of strategic significance. Other sub-processes include new product development, branding, positioning and pricing.

The third key process in a demand system is value delivery. This is to do with how value is communicated and conveyed by an organization to a

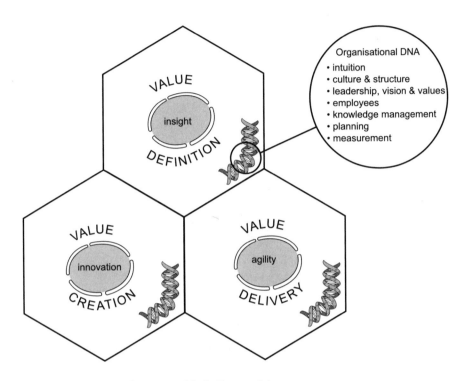

Figure 0.1 The New Consumer Marketing model

specific audience. Media and channels obviously play a role alongside service, technology integration and supply-chain management. The watchword here is organizational agility.

The seven elements needed to make a demand system viable are described as the organizational DNA. The interrelationships of intuition, culture and structure, leadership, vision and values, employees, knowledge management, planning, and measurement work within the cells to optimize performance and ensure competitive survival.

The New Consumer Marketing model, therefore, lifts marketing out of its crisis in terms of presenting a conceptual guide for practitioners for generating and managing the exchange process under conditions of competition. The model provides a framework that enables an organization to describe and position its marketing strategy. In doing this, it identifies the consumer segments it seeks to serve, determining where and how it will compete.

OVERVIEW OF THE BOOK

The structure of this book is outlined below.

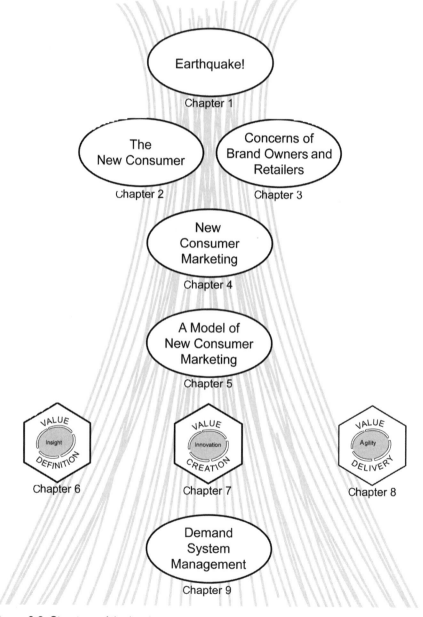

Figure 0.2 Structure of the book

Chapter 1 provides an overview of the changing competitive landscape and places marketing within the business context. Chapter 2 describes the profile of New Consumers, highlighting the challenges they pose to business. Chapter 3 then explores the concerns of brand owners and retailers, who, in the face of change, must meet these challenges in order to survive.

Chapter 4 introduces New Consumer Marketing as an emerging business discipline. New Consumer Marketing is not simply another way of managing the marketing mix, but a viable means of addressing the range of issues that enable an organization to compete successfully in a particular market. Its key objective is to help the organization establish sustainable competitive advantage by means of superior performance. High levels of performance are achieved and maintained through the processes of value definition, value creation and value delivery.

A framework for conceptualizing New Consumer Marketing as the management of a demand system is presented in Chapter 5. Chapters 6, 7 and 8 then focus on each of the three key processes that form the working 'cells' of the New Consumer Marketing model: value definition, value creation and value delivery. The concluding chapter, Chapter 9, identifies the elements that make up the organizational DNA – the genetic code that drives the cells' performance and determines the overall success of the demand system.

References to source material and Notes on further reading are to be found at the back of the book.

Earthquake!

(2008)

1

The current crisis in marketing is underscored by profound change in the marketing environment.

A new marketplace is emerging and bringing with it a host of challenges never before encountered. For marketers, this event is both exciting and unnerving: opportunities for innovation and growth parallel threats to proven methodologies and the status quo. The challenges posed by the changing competitive arena are not restricted to a particular industry or sector, but span the gamut of enterprises operating today. All businesses are being affected to some degree by the root-and-branch upheaval that is occurring in the wider marketing environment. At the start of the third millennium, a paradigm shift in commerce is clear: we have moved from a production-driven to a consumption-led economy.

While the forces of demand and supply continue to regulate the economy, the nature of the exchange has altered beyond all recognition. The 'them and us' adversarial approach to trade is giving way to consumer involvement in all aspects of product and service development and delivery. Supplying organizations use increasingly clever methods to woo consumer loyalty and maintain competitive edge. High-powered and dynamic data technology helps produce finely tuned marketing strategies, which can be implemented on a one-to-one basis through an ever-expanding choice of traditional and electronic media. Customers and consumers exploit this greater access to information and the ability to achieve dialogue with suppliers, exercising their new found empowerment by increasingly leveraging sales propositions in their own favour. The result is a mutually influenced, beneficial interaction.

This radical transition in the way commercial transactions are conducted is evident no more so than in the rise of the buyer–seller *relationship*. Managing an ongoing relationship is an entirely different matter to managing a single transaction, and the challenge for marketers today is compounded by the growing complexity of the context in which it takes place. Marketing, especially consumer marketing, faces a daunting prospect: quickly undergo profound change or prepare for certain death.

MARKETING IN CRISIS

> ... there was a moment of pregnant stillness, then a sibilant whisper, a sort of faint seismic exhalation, and then the world lurched.
>
> Ben Macintyre, *The Times*, 23 March 2002

This is the description a journalist gave after experiencing a major earthquake. If one had been listening in the mid-1990s, they would have heard similar rumblings throughout the marketing profession. An article published in the *McKinsey Quarterly* in 1993 claimed: 'Many consumer goods CEOs are beginning to think that marketing is no longer delivering', suggesting that 'marketers are simply not picking up the right signals any more'. A Coopers & Lybrand survey of the same year found comparable consensus among senior executives within fast moving consumer goods (fmcg), retail and service sector organizations. Quoting their non-marketing managers, respondents expressed concern about the role and value of marketing: 'Marketing is increasingly living a lie in my organization', 'If marketing departments disappeared, would anybody notice? Would it really matter?'.

A growing number of articles on the subject of marketing then appeared in the media, stimulating debate among academics and practitioners as to whether or not this 'bad press' was warranted. In late 1993, the UK's Chartered Institute of Marketing (CIM) commissioned a report on the future of marketing in key British enterprises (Chartered Institute of Marketing, 1994). Boldly entitled *The Challenge of Change*, the CIM investigation into marketing's performance and promise delivered mixed tidings. A multitude of research reports and commentaries from preceding decades as well as the then current clutch revealed that marketing was set to become increasingly relevant and strategically important as a management function but that it remained, on the whole, poorly executed in Britain.

The last decade of the twentieth century was symbolically brought to a close with a decisive report by the Marketing Forum, the UK's leading authority on the role and status of marketing. With the objectives of identifying the key drivers and core responsibilities of the marketing discipline, the report sought to address the growing unease among marketers. Original research attempted to answer the following questions:

- In the post-dotcom boom, what are the new drivers of marketing focus?
- How does the arrival of the information era affect how we, as marketers, operate?
- What is our remit now and what new responsibilities can we expect to assume in future?

From the strength of response, the message was clear: the conventional tools of marketing were no longer applicable and there was a pressing need for fresh thinking. The research showed that marketing appeared to be losing its way, thrown off course by the myriad of unprecedented pressures and developments in the now global marketplace. It was felt that the future of marketing, if there was to be one, rested firmly on the adoption of new approaches and new attitudes. While the underlying principles of marketing remained, for the most part, intact, the practical tools and techniques employed required radical revision.

Traditional marketing devices such as the 4Ps (product, place, price and promotion) had emerged in the production-driven era of the 1950s–1970s. The subsequent globalization of market activity and explosion in the availability and use of new-wave technologies, particularly the Internet, to name but two key drivers of change, turned the existing business premise on its head. Instead of being the focus of persuasion to buy what producers wished to produce, consumers became the focus of production itself; they could influence to a great extent the nature of products. Business prosperity relied on retaining valuable customer relationships, not revving the engines of production.

To grasp the full weight of this seismic shift in the rules of commercial engagement, it is useful to look back briefly at the development of marketing as an established management discipline. Its evolution is suffused with hard lessons and valuable learning. Only by understanding marketing's role at different points in time can we anchor the debate about its future in a meaningful context.

THE EVOLUTION OF MARKETING

While the application of marketing has existed since people first traded with one another, its emergence as a distinct business discipline has happened relatively recently in the period between the First and Second World Wars. In the UK, for example, modern-day marketing became synonymous with brand marketing as practised in the 1950s and 1960s by fmcg companies such as Unilever and Procter & Gamble. Marketing stood for a business philosophy based on meeting the needs of customers and creating sustainable competitive advantage. It was supported by a business function bearing the same name.

Marketers drew on an operational framework rooted in the 4Ps, and the most knowledgeable had at their disposal an expanding toolbox of conceptual, diagnostic and predictive tools. It is worth considering some of these briefly to appreciate marketing's integral role. The product life cycle (PLC), introduced in 1950, promulgated the notion that products pass through typical phases, from 'launch' to 'maturity' to 'decline' and finally 'exit' from the marketplace. The PLC was followed by a range of models developed by rival management consultancies, such as the Boston Consulting Group (BCG) and McKinsey & Co., to aid the marketer in the management of both single products and product portfolios. The most enduring of these analytical devices are BCG's Boston Matrix, and McKinsey's Directional Policy Matrix (DPM) designed in conjunction with General Electric in the USA and Shell in Europe.

The four-box Boston Matrix (see Figure 1.1a) considered products in terms of their relative market share and market growth rate. It held that the perfect conglomerate needed a mix of three types of product. Profit from the steady earners ('cash cows') could be used to invest in products with huge growth potential ('stars') and underwrite those under development ('question marks'). The fourth quadrant of the matrix was allocated to product failures ('dogs'), whose poor performance or excessive cash consumption justifies their being discarded altogether. The DPM (see Figure 1.1b) expanded the number of variables used in the Boston Matrix, adding market attractiveness and business strengths in order to analyse product performance in greater depth.

As marketing tools and techniques aimed at understanding product behaviour became more refined, the need to understand consumer

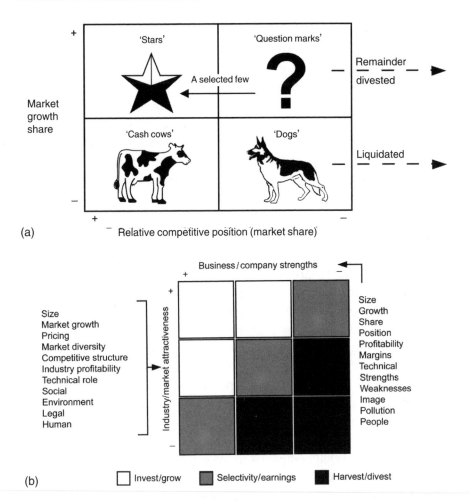

Figure 1.1 (a) The Boston Matrix and (b) the Directional Policy Matrix
Cranfield School of Management 'Marketing Management: A relationship marketing perspective', 2000
reproduced with permission of Palgrave Macmillan

behaviour became more pronounced. Demand in consumer markets in the 1950s and 1960s was buoyant due to rising levels of disposable income and the influence of new forms of communication, notably television. Marketing was harnessed as a means of persuading masses of consumers to buy what was manufactured, and the 'make–sell' philosophy of business established itself as consonant with the production-driven era.

The guiding principle for developing mass consumer markets was to acquire ever-greater numbers of consumers and take maximum market share.

This strategy was underpinned by research from PIMS (Profit Impact of Market Strategy), which showed that the greater the market share achieved, the bigger the profits that would accrue to the company. The pace and scope of mass marketing were set by the American consumer goods giants, for whom the market appeared to be an ever-climbing sales curve, until the world was jolted out of this misapprehension by a series of oil crises in the 1970s. The consequent international economic downturn, followed by high inflation at home, had a serious impact on consumers. Consumer spending habits displayed prudence and sophistication in much larger measure.

The Rise of Relationship Marketing

Supplying organizations responded to the constrained economic environment of the 1970s by re-examining what they were offering to customers. To increase product appeal, differentiation and value for money, many augmented their product offerings by incorporating a service element. This spawned the development of services marketing as a business function. In mature markets where the rate of growth had slowed or even stopped, it became more difficult for organizations to pursue a strategy of gaining market share. With the pool of new prospects diminished, marketing attention steered towards retaining and growing existing customer relationships. Consequently, 'customer loyalty' achieved priority, and its prime strategic importance remains to this day.

The shift in marketing emphasis from customer acquisition to customer retention became enshrined in the principles of Relationship Marketing (RM). RM, unlike transaction marketing, recognizes that commercial transactions are not isolated events but that they take place within a live and continuous context of engagement – a 'relationship' between buyer and seller. Underpinning the idea of an enduring and potentially 'growable' relationship with a customer is the concept of customer value: that is, the customer has an intrinsic and dynamic value to the supplying organization and vice versa.

Measures of marketing success then turned from numbers of customers (market share) to share of customer expenditure (share of 'wallet') and potential customer value (customer lifetime value). The work of Bain consultants Frederick Reichheld and Earl Sasser was seminal in demonstrating the large impact on profitability of small increases in customer retention rates. Further research by Reichheld and Teal (1996), showing the increasing profitability of customers the longer the relationship lasts, added strength to the argument for a relationship marketing approach.

Issues surrounding RM implementation were less clear, and business theorists usually advocated relationship building via the identification of a number of key groups or market domains. For example, the Multiple Markets Model developed by Christopher, Payne and Ballantyne (1991, 2002) recommends that marketing activity should be focused on six main markets:

1. consumer markets (or customer markets in the business-to-business sector);
2. internal markets, i.e. employees;
3. supplier and alliance markets, e.g. business partners, suppliers, consultants, contractors;
4. influencer markets, e.g. venture capitalists, regulators, lobbyists and litigators;
5. referral markets, e.g. customer advocates, intermediaries, business advisors;
6. recruitment markets, e.g. employment agencies, graduates, the pool of potential employees.

This multiple-markets approach embraces a more holistic view of the marketplace. It forces marketers to think beyond managing one market made up of consumers (or customers) and extends the marketing mix to include the increasingly important elements of people, process and the provision of customer service.

As RM became more widely accepted during the 1990s, developments continued apace in IT and computational methodologies, resulting in the convergence of database marketing and customer service delivery. This led to the concept of Customer Relationship Management (CRM).

The Test of CRM[1]

CRM was the last big idea of the twentieth century to grab the attention of marketers. It appeared to present the magic formula for marketing success – the opportunity to galvanize the business behind a marketing-led

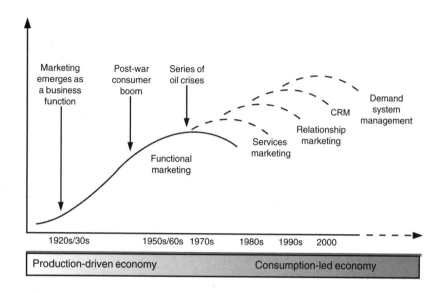

Figure 1.2 The marketing life cycle

strategy. Moreover, as commentators have observed, it offered 'the mystique of new technologies and a new three letter acronym'. The theory behind CRM is that managing customer relationships is an integrated business process involving the consolidation of individual customer data from multiple sources to create a mutually valuable proposition. CRM's emphasis on using IT to monitor customers' transaction histories and exploit their purchasing behaviour serves to reinforce the impact of customer retention strategies. With real-time access to customer-specific information, organizations can segment customers by value, target marketing strategies towards the most promising opportunities, and personalize marketing communications. Consequently, service levels are guided by customer profitability. CRM seemed to provide, at last, the means of implementing RM effectively and, as an incremental development, served to extend the marketing life cycle (see Figure 1.2).

Investment in CRM systems across Europe is such that it is one of the fastest growing markets in the IT industry. However, those organizations that interpreted CRM as simply the purchase of an expensive software program found little succour in the smart new technology. It has been claimed that up to 97% of CRM installations fail to deliver the anticipated benefits. Problems stem from a lack of clarity about what CRM actually is and how to implement it successfully. For some it has meant better marketing communications, providing a means of escaping from the constraints of mass communications and of achieving more personalized dialogue. Others have taken a broader view, using the terms CRM and marketing almost interchangeably. A third school of thought has highlighted the IT aspect, regarding CRM as the technological enhancement of business processes. Each interpretation of CRM offers an equal number of implementation models and, with so many options and interpretations, it is little wonder that CRM has failed to meet expectations.

Current research shows that there are a number of preconditions that need to be satisfied prior to implementing a CRM strategy. Organizations must have a clearly defined marketing strategy in place, IT systems that are aligned to the goals of the marketing strategy, and an organizational culture which ably supports the implementation of CRM. A misalignment in any of these relationships leads to a failure of CRM, creating waste and disappointing performance.

It is clear that most CRM systems are not conceived with the active, demanding, IT-literate consumer in mind. Their main focus is on providing information about the customer to the company. They seldom offer the consumer direct access to information about the supplier or vendor or their own account. As business theorist Patricia Seybold asserts, 'CRM systems should be designed with customers as the design center. Customers should have the ability to maintain (though not the responsibility of maintaining) information related to their relationships' (Seybold et al., 2001). This view is in keeping with the prediction of research firm Gartner that by 2005 consumers will start to take control of their own data. Together, these assertions suggest that CMR – or customer-managed relationships – rather than CRM, should be the guiding notion in devising relationship management systems.

Whether or not CRM survives as a formal discipline, it has been a valuable step in marketing's development. It has established the business case for adopting the customer's perspective and involving the customer in the formulation of product and service strategies. The timing of this realization is no coincidence; it is a creative response to the eruption of dramatic change within the macro-marketing environment.

CHANGES IN THE MACRO-MARKETING ENVIRONMENT[2]

The present trend towards more customer-centric ways of doing business is being propelled and directed by a fundamental change in the marketing environment. Using the earthquake metaphor, the two 'tectonic plates' that shape the marketing landscape are the production-driven economy and the consumption-led economy. As our manufacturing base declines we can see that it is consumption, and not production, which is emerging as the central motor of contemporary society.

Of course, we have to look at production and consumption as two sides of the same coin. Production does not take place without a corresponding level of consumption, and, similarly, no consumption can take place unless something is produced. For some supplying organizations, the boundary between these two sets of activities erodes and they fuse into what Alvin Toffler so presciently described as 'prosumption' in his best-seller *Future Shock*. As long ago as 1970, Toffler foresaw that consumers would soon be faced with the greatest variety of unstandardized goods and services ever seen. He believed this increasing diversity of products would be encouraged by two economic factors: 'First, consumers have more money to lavish on their specialized wants; second, and even more important, *as technology becomes more sophisticated, the cost of introducing variations declines*' [his italics].

Today, leading organizations such as Lands' End, Dell, Procter & Gamble and Pearson, the TV company, demonstrate the wisdom of Toffler's vision:

- Clothing retailer Lands' End started offering online tailoring in October 2000 in the USA. A year later the company claimed that 40% of all chino and jeans sales on its website were custom orders. Customers would enter their measurements onscreen, including their weight, height and hip–thigh proportions. An inbuilt computer program would analyse the information given and calculate the ideal dimensions of the trousers. The order specifications would be sent direct to a manufacturing plant in Mexico, where the fabric pattern would be produced by a computerized cutting machine and then passed to a sewing machinist. Two to four weeks after the order was placed, the customer would receive the trousers.

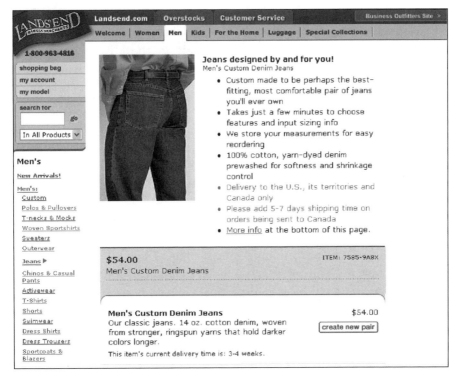

Figure 1.3 Lands' End.com online tailoring
Reproduced by permission of LandsEnd

- Dell, one of *Fortune* magazine's top ten 'most admired' companies, designs, manufactures and customizes computing products and services to customers' requirements. Using the online 'Configure & Buy' facility, customers can create the computer system that best meets their needs by a process of selecting options from drop-down menus. As they do so, the total price changes accordingly at the bottom of their screen.

- Procter & Gamble has a website called 'Community Corner' that it uses to build relationships with consumers, or marketing partners as they are known internally. The website is an online forum in which consumers can talk about existing brands, suggest ideas and changes, and contribute to surveys. There is also a chance for people with patents for new products to discuss them with Procter & Gamble.

- The television programme *Pop Idol*, created by Pearson, enabled viewers to vote in their favourite pop star from a preselected shortlist.

In the final show of the UK series nine million viewers voted by telephone, awarding Will Young celebrity status. Young then achieved the fastest-selling debut single in the UK, as more than 1.1 million fans went out to buy the record by the star they had created. The programme's format has since been adopted by television producers in the USA, with similar success.

The predominance of a consumption-led economy is reflected in a number of macro market statistics. For example, in the UK the proportion of gross domestic product (GDP) provided by manufacturing has been on a downward trend since the mid-1970s. This position is reflected in each of the G7 industrialized economies (Germany, France, Italy, Japan, Canada, the USA, and the UK). In the case of the UK, manufacturing accounted for around one third of the economy's total output in 1960. However, by the start of the new millennium this had fallen to less than one fifth, with only the USA showing a fall below this figure. This has been driven in part by the allocation of an increasing proportion of disposable income to expenditure on a wide range of services and luxury goods. Sectors such as banking, tourism, leisure, entertainment and telecommunications have been the main beneficiaries.

This economic position is mirrored in employment patterns. Significant job losses are expected in the primary sector of the economy (agriculture, mining and utilities) over the next couple of years, while manufacturing can expect to lose around 80,000 employees each year between 2000 and 2005, when the loss is expected to slow to 50,000 employees per annum. The decline in engineering will be seen as the biggest contributor to these losses. On the other hand, distribution, hotels, the transport sector and communications can expect an increase of 40,000 new jobs annually to 2005. However, the biggest job increases are expected to come in other market sectors, where growth in professional services in particular will mean an increase of around 140,000 new jobs each year to 2005.

Not surprisingly, these employment trends find equal expression in qualification statistics. The number of students graduating in engineering and technology are down by 9%, from 35,700 to 32,400 over the period 1997 to 2001. In contrast, degrees received in law and the arts both show increases. Graduates in business and administration now dominate the job market, growing from 61,700 in 1997 to 65,300 in 2001. Those with degrees in creative arts and design, however, show the biggest proportionate jump, from 24,800 in 1997 to 29,500 in 2001.

These facts and figures stress the fundamental change in market dynamics, from a production to a consumption focus. Consumption and the servicing of consumption increasingly form the basis of business planning. The economic sector becomes ever more tightly tied to businesses that have an asset base made up of intangible services, as opposed to hard and fast production. This shift has significant ramifications for marketers – consumer marketers in particular – who need actively to acknowledge that new ways of thinking and operating are needed if we are to meet unrivalled market and management demands.

IMPLICATIONS FOR CONSUMER MARKETING

A substantial amount of soul searching has gone on in marketing circles over the past decade as marketing's role and contribution to business performance have been challenged by both change and a lack of it. The diminished sense of influence, power and value among marketing practitioners, and shared frustration about what to do next, is rooted in the fact that the certainties of the production-driven economy have been replaced with the uncertainties of the consumption-led economy and marketing thinking has not kept pace. The tools, techniques and theories taught in business schools today largely promote a mechanistic approach to marketing, which, as the following chapters will show, is not relevant to the organic nature of present-day trade relations.

While Relationship Marketing, and its offshoot Customer Relationship Management, have revolutionized marketing practice, much more needs to be done to manage the matching of supply and demand synergistically. Marketers, whose role has always been located at the critical interface between buyers and sellers, are well placed to lead the thought process. Consumer markets, especially, offer valuable insight and testing ground for the development of more appropriate concepts and codes of practice. There the customer base is usually more numerous, remote and capricious, and the use of intermediaries is commonplace. As the tremors shaking the marketing landscape grow stronger and more frequent, the imperative to find new meaning for marketers becomes an unenviable, unavoidable and urgent responsibility.

SUMMARY POINTS

- Marketers are operating in a context of fundamental transition. The certainties of the production-driven economy have been replaced by the uncertainties of the consumption-led economy.

- Consumption and the servicing of consumption now form the central motor of contemporary society.

- Many of the conventional tools and techniques of marketing, developed mainly in the production-driven era, no longer apply and marketing's contribution to business is increasingly unclear.

- Relationship Marketing moved marketing focus from customer acquisition to customer retention.

- The implementation of Relationship Marketing through CRM systems has been largely unsuccessful, and there is an outstanding requirement for greater clarity in terms of CRM definition and practice.

- Consumer markets offer insight and testing ground for the future development of marketing.

The New Consumer 2

Consumption and consumption management are being redefined by the New Consumer.

Consumption (the act or process of consuming) has always been a characteristic of human nature. But consumption as it relates to consuming goods and services that do not merely fulfil needs but satisfy wants and desires is a modern-day development, one that accelerated after the Second World War. Since then a growing range of businesses have come to see their interactions with consumers as the execution of a formalized process of consumption. They have engaged the marketing profession to hone this process to optimum effect. In parallel with this development, consumer rights have evolved to the point where the advocacy of consumer interests is no longer the sole remit of consumer organizations: consumers themselves are leading the cause.

In order to manage the process of consumption effectively in the context of transition described in Chapter 1, marketers, traditionally, have adopted the classic marketing approach of the 4Ps (product, place, price and promotion). They have used these elements of the marketing mix to facilitate their command-and-control philosophy. However, the advent of a new kind of consumer is showing this traditional marketing approach to be out of date. 'New Consumers' are well informed and highly empowered. They are increasingly influencing the shape and form of products and services, as well as the future of market players.

CONSUMPTION IN TRANSFORMATION

'Consumption' is often considered a contemporary word, whose arrival was marked by the conspicuous consumption patterns of the 1980s. Yet some commentators point to an earlier era: the 1950s, when the Marshall Plan helped to rebuild Europe. The economic boom that followed the Second World War, lasting some 25 years, ensured that many members of the lower social classes could have all sorts of goods and services their parents could only dream of.

Other commentators look still further back. Sociologist Grant McCracken (1988), for example, turns to the reign of Queen Elizabeth I of England and the prosperity of the last quarter of the sixteenth century.[1] At that time, an explosion of consumerist behaviour was fuelled by members of a social elite who became caught up in a 'riot of consumption' as they vied for the attention of the monarch. The accumulation of expenses by noblemen at court meant they had less to spend on their families – and a new phenomenon was born. The individual, rather than the family, began to feature as the basic unit of consumption, motivated rather more by a sense of buying for the here-and-now than for the longer term.

The beginnings of consumer society might also be found in the wave of economic prosperity that hit eighteenth-century England and prompted the emergence of a middle class. For these consumers, the possession of fashionable goods represented an important index of their social standing. Moreover, new marketing and advertising techniques accompanied these different patterns of buying behaviour by new groups of consumers.

Expansion of the Consumer Concept

Regardless of where in time we position the first signs of consumption, what is important is to acknowledge its pervasive influence. The concept of the consumer, and the building of businesses around it, is no longer confined to those who produce 'things', i.e. manufacturers. Organizations as diverse as charities, utilities suppliers, government bodies and even religious orders have become attuned to thinking of the individuals they interact with as consumers.

British Gas

British Gas was privatized in 1986 and demerged from British Gas plc in 1997. Today, it is part of Centrica, the holding company for a range of businesses, including the AA, Goldfish and One.Tel in the UK, and Energy America and Luminus overseas. For most consumers of gas fuel, it is an unexciting product. Their gas-fired stoves break down, and the bills always seem disproportionately large to the burning small flame in their boilers. As a part of Centrica, British Gas set out to turn around a loss-making operation, optimize the use of its sales force and maintain brand presence. Now the business is highly profitable: the result of a strategy that has included detailed work on customer segmentation and the use of marketing campaigns to smooth out peaks and troughs in consumer demand for maintenance and installation.

Caldey Island

On Caldey Island off the Welsh coast, a group of Cistercian monks is developing an e-business in an attempt to make the monastery financially self-sufficient. The brothers produce a range of perfumes, bath oils, hand creams and men's aftershaves, as well as shortbread made to an old recipe. The idea of a web shop grew from the problem of geographical remoteness: the holy island is only accessible by licensed boat services between the months of April and October, making for a short selling season. Early indications are that the site (www.caldey-island.co.uk) is succeeding.

Defence of Consumer Rights

Alongside the growth in consumer numbers, products and expenditure, there has been growth in a consciousness of consumer rights. The process of advancing the cause of consumers' interests in relation to the producer or supplying organization is known as *consumerism* and should be seen as distinct from *consumption*, or the act of consuming the products and services produced.

The 'consumer movement', loosely defined as the ongoing campaign to secure consumer rights, began in the late 1950s and early 1960s, when an increasing interest in consumer and environmental issues seeded the idea that consumers possess the power to influence manufacturers (and subsequently, many others, such as retailers and service providers).[2] The UK Consumers' Association, founded in 1957, set out to emulate the American Consumers' Union (CU). Within a few years, consumers' associations had formed in several other European countries, notably Holland and Belgium. All were based on the CU model of an organization carrying out product tests and making public the results to inform consumers (see Figure 2.1). The consumer voice was given further impetus by President John F. Kennedy's groundbreaking address to Congress in

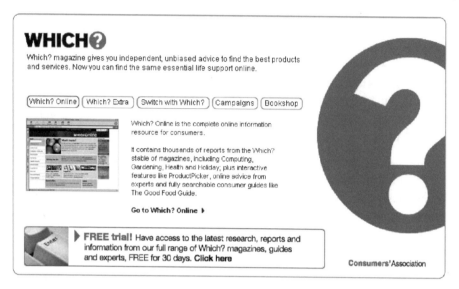

Figure 2.1 Which? online

Which? Published by Consumers' Association, 2 Marlybone Road, London NW1 4DF, for further information please call 0800 252 100

March 1962, where he asserted the rights of consumers 'to safety, to be informed, to choose and to be heard'.

Today, consumer advocacy no longer resides solely with consumer groups. The language of consumer rights has entered the corporate world. 'When people pay money for a brand or to a company, they feel they are buying rights to how they are treated – rights to be respected, treated honestly and fairly, and to have their points of view appreciated.' This was a comment made by Lucy Purdy, planning director at Publicis, when her communications agency published its findings on consumer attitudes to registering complaints about poor goods and services.

In order to create a business culture that meets these expectations on the part of the consumer, Mohanibar Sawhney and Philip Kotler from Kellogg University advocate implementing a Customer Bill of Rights for the Information Age (Sawhney and Kotler, 2001). Their proposed draft bill supports a consumer right to anonymity, to be remembered, and to share in pay-offs, among other things. They warn that 'Violating these fundamental rights, while tempting and even profitable in the short run, will be disastrous in the long run'.

CONSUMPTION MANAGEMENT IN QUESTION

The management of consumption has traditionally been undertaken through the adoption of the 'make–sell' approach characteristic of the production-driven economy described in Chapter 1. Supplying organizations (i.e. manufacturers) made things and it was the task of the marketer to persuade consumers to buy them. Their instruments of persuasion were the 4Ps. The challenge for these organizations was to satisfy customer needs by producing the right product at the right price, making it available in the right place at the right time, and promoting its winning features through the right means of communication.

This mechanistic model of consumption management was later enhanced by the principles of Relationship Marketing (RM), born out of a focus on services marketing. RM stressed that the management of consumption was about far more than simply putting products into the marketplace. The dawning realization that a manufacturer is not so much a product company but a service company with a product offering introduced the idea of building relationships with consumers over time, based on meeting their needs in relation to both the functional aspects of the product and the more intangible aspects of the service elements.

In parallel with this development, a growing consciousness of consumer rights and consumer power has created more confident consumers, ones who are finding their voice and have at their disposal the means of expressing it. At the point of confluence of these two trends – RM on the one hand, and consumer rights on the other – the way in which consumption is managed comes under question. The 'make–sell' approach, enhanced through RM, does not meet with the expectations of this new, empowered consumer. Organizations need to acknowledge this change and devise new ways of managing consumption based on consumers themselves.

A NEW KIND OF CONSUMER

The present consumer-driven marketplace is characterized by a new kind of consumer, one who has been variously described as 'active', 'knowledgeable' and 'post-modern'.[3] In essence, this is a 'New Consumer', a creature distinctly different and identifiable from its predecessors.

Marketers need to develop a deep understanding of the attitudes and behaviours of this New Consumer, if they are to break away from the mechanistic models of the production-driven era and develop a relevant approach to exploiting the business potential of current consumer culture. New Consumers possess a number of distinguishing features, the most significant of which are highlighted here.

New Consumers Are Exercised By Time

The first step in understanding changing cultures of consumption is to recognize the different ways in which New Consumers relate to the concept of time. Time has become a precious commodity, and many products and services reflect this insight, capitalizing on the time-poor/cash-rich trade-off many consumers make. Consumers with little time and high levels of disposable income have become 'outsourcers' – their clothes go to the dry cleaners, nannies look after their children, cleaners and tradespeople keep their house in good order, and so on. Businesses that have spotted this market niche include enterprising property developers whose new-build homes come fitted with fake lawns and supermarkets which offer pre-packaged, pre-cooked, ready-made meals. Personal full-service agency Enviego goes further and has created a PA (personal assistant) service that will take care of everything from actively remembering birthdays to organizing walking the dog.

Contemporary consumer behaviour also illustrates that consumers appear to either actively embrace the pace of change and the constant stream of new products and services, or want to run and hide. The former are living life to the max and desirous of anything but routine. These 'time tourists' give themselves away by their pursuit of agelessness, disregard for gender boundaries, and delight in the finer things in life. For brand owners, time tourists represent new markets and marketing opportunities. Clinique, for example, cleverly acknowledges male buyers with the advertisement: 'Don't say the word "cosmetics". Clinique's "Skin supplies for men"' (see Figure 2.2a).

'Time refugees', on the other hand, display characteristics best described as defensive in the face of the pace of change. These consumers seek security and a sense of belonging. They want to find and maintain a home, be it spiritual or physical. They want to feel part of a community and form

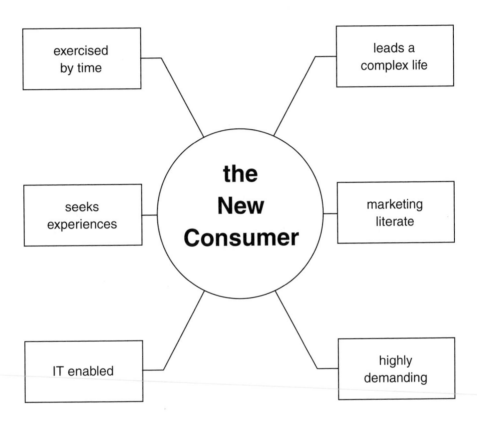

Figure 2.2 The New Consumer

relationship bonds with other people. Buying certain brands therefore becomes a way of linking with like-minded consumers. The worldwide marketing success of Harley-Davidson and its 600,000-strong Harley Owners' Group demonstrates this drive to belong to a tribe or group. For some time refugees, purchases become a sort of reward. L'Oreal, for example, targets this group with the strapline: 'Because you're worth it' (see Figure 2.2b). Time refugees are looking to anchor themselves in a transient world. The website, www.friendsreunited.com, which reunites former school friends, has successfully captured their imagination.

New Consumers Lead Complex Lives

The marketplace of the New Consumer is highly fragmented and this is in large part due to the highly complex lives consumers lead. On one level, they display multiple personalities, seeming to dip in and out of different stereotypic personality types. The prevalence of this consumer behaviour was exemplified by a piece of advice from *Cosmopolitan* magazine to its female readership: 'Be an it-girl on Saturday, a kitten on Sunday, a career woman on Monday, a devoted girlfriend on Tuesday …'. It is as if consumers can take on chameleon-like properties and adapt their projected personas to suit the situation.

This complex behaviour creates problems for marketers whose segmentation analyses are constructed on the premise that consumers can be categorized permanently in one of a number of predefined 'boxes'. However, in displaying multiple personalities, consumers can appear to occupy a number of different boxes depending on the occasion. For example, in the airline industry, a passenger might choose to fly business class or first class for business travel, economy class for family holidays, and with a special ticket (discount or promotion) for a long weekend. Designing a marketing strategy to capture or keep this customer is an almost impossible task if simple demographics are used as the basis. Making sense of this apparent chaos requires marketers to abandon their need for certainty, and to develop a tolerance of ambiguity and a skill in adaptability. In addition to recognizing consumers' changing attitudes to time, marketers must respect their preferences and different needs and desires.

New Consumers Seek Experiences

Marketing theorists have for some time pointed out that consumers don't buy product features, they buy product benefits. As marketing guru Theodore Levitt famously commented: 'Customers don't buy ¼ inch drills, they buy ¼ inch holes'. In the case of New Consumers, their purchasing behaviour is further distinguished by the desire to buy an 'experience'. It is now possible to purchase such an experience off the shelf in high street retailers. W H Smith, for example, offers them in a catalogue. Their range includes a day driving a Ferrari or a JCB, a visit to a health farm, and a photographic makeover. Prices range from £99.99 to £2,999.99: the latter buys the thrill of diving with sharks in South Africa. Children under 17 years of age are offered their own choice of 'first' experiences, such as driving a car or being a TV presenter.

In response to this desire to 'consume' experiences, many retailers have moved from simply offering ranges of products to also offering ranges of experiences. In the pub market, for example, consumers can enjoy an Irish pub experience one evening, followed by an Australian bar experience the next, and an American bar experience resembling the television sit-com *Cheers* after that. Except that these experiences are not 'real' in the sense of being non-contrived. Instead, they are formulaic and themed; reality is deliberately blurred with hyper-reality.

US consultants Joseph Pine and James Gilmore (1998; see also Pine and Gilmore, 1999) describe this 'experience economy' as one where 'Instead of relying on our own wherewithal to experience the new and wondrous – as has been done for ages – we will increasingly pay companies to stage experiences for us, just as we now pay companies for services we once delivered ourselves, goods we once made ourselves, and commodities we once extracted ourselves'. Clearly, consumer offerings and marketing messages addressed to New Consumers must take this trend on board.

New Consumers Are Marketing Literate and Highly Demanding

The command-and-control philosophy traditionally adopted by marketers to manage the consumption process is inappropriate today. As every marketer who engages consumers in research will know, consumers are becoming more marketing literate and less easy to please. They can deconstruct marketing activities with almost as much insight as most marketers. For example, the average consumer can quickly sort the daily post into three piles: personal mail, business mail and unsolicited, or 'junk', mail. They are capable of identifying each without even opening the envelope.

Consumers are no longer passive absorbers of marketing messages. In the words of author Alan Mitchell (2001), 'The observed have started playing games with the observer'. At one extreme, these 'games' take the form of protests and demonstrations against globalization, such as the disruption of the World Trade negotiations in Seattle in 1999 and the G8 summit in Genoa in 2001. Naomi Klein's book *No Logo: Taking Aim at the Brand Bullies* (2000), is another example. It is a highly acclaimed assessment of multinational brand-name corporations, labour abuses and anti-corporate resistance, which quickly became the bible of the anti-globalization movement after its publication in the USA.

At the other extreme, consumers make their views known in less violent ways. For example, those who are unhappy with their purchases and intent upon standing up for their rights can turn to consumer watchdogs and other advocacy groups which operate through traditional as well as electronic media. In fact, consumer redress has become a source of 'infotainment' – part information and part entertainment. Consumers also have the wherewithal to take direct action, such as setting up 'vigilante' websites. Marketers should monitor these sites carefully as they can provide a rich seam of consumer feedback. Equally, their impact on consumer and corporate perception should be managed carefully. In 1999 Dunkin' Donuts, the fast food retailer, bought out the 'gripe site' set up two years earlier by a customer who had been upset at the absence of any skimmed milk for his coffee.

Such consumer activity reflects a knowledge on the part of consumers about how marketing works and a new-found confidence in expressing dissatisfaction. It is imperative, therefore, that the New Consumer be equally involved in the consumption management process, and that a partnership of open dialogue and mutual respect be developed between the trading parties.

New Consumers Are IT Enabled

Underpinning the way New Consumers live their lives and make and use their purchases are, of course, developments in information technology

(IT). This fundamental feature of the New Consumer raises issues for marketers about how to connect with consumers who live in a technologically interactive and integrated world. The exponential growth in the use of mobile phones (devices first developed by Bell Laboratories in the 1940s) has presented particular challenges. Consumers worldwide have needed little persuading of the benefits of the mobile phone, which, unlike landline systems, links people rather than locations. In the UK, 28 million people owned mobile handsets in 2001 and this figure is predicted to rise to 40.5 million by 2005, according to research firm Gartner. The fundamental appeal of the mobile phone is that it extends a basic human quality – the ability to communicate. Teenagers, in particular, have become the main conduits through which mobile phones have found their way into wider society, and they were also the first group to realize the potential of text messaging. The Japanese teenage generation has even been dubbed, *oya yubi sedai*, meaning the thumb tribe, on account of the dexterity with which they text message.

Throughout this growth in mobile phone ownership, consumers have shown themselves to be one step ahead of marketers, who have yet to really demonstrate that they understand the market drivers and how this mobile channel can be most effectively integrated into the communications mix. Equipped with mobile phones and other handheld mobile devices, consumers are no longer static and fixed in time and space relative to brands. They have a choice of channels through which to connect with a brand and will exercise individual preference in using them. For example, consumers may prefer to purchase some categories of goods online, such as CDs, videos, books and software, but use the Internet to browse for other products and services. In the US it is estimated that only 1% of new cars are purchased online, while half of the nation's car buyers use the Internet solely to research and compare automotive product options.

IMPLICATIONS FOR CONSUMER MARKETING

In today's consumption-led economy, using the 4Ps (or even the 7Ps of a Relationship Marketing approach) as the basis for marketing strategy misses a fundamental point: consumption is enacted by consumers and therefore they – and not products – should be the starting point of marketing strategy origination. Robert Lauterborn (1991) described the need to focus instead on the 4Cs: consumer needs and wants, costs to the consumer (time, money, effort etc.), convenience factors, and communication (how the consumer wishes to be communicated with by the supplying organization). With the arrival of the New Consumer, the command-and-control approach to consumption management, so typical of the production-driven era, is no longer applicable.

Marketers need to accept that the marketplace is no longer stable and predictable but is instead dynamic and complex, and, as a consequence, their need for certainty must become replaced by a tolerance of ambiguity. This is driven, for the most part, by the heterogeneity of the New Consumer. Consumers today no longer resemble the conventional perceptions formed in the era of mass marketing, and traditional approaches to consumer research and segmentation do not adequately capture their essence. New Consumers have minds of their own and are not reluctant to make their views known. New Consumers are empowered to make their purchases through an ever-expanding choice of media and channels. Moreover, they change suppliers easily, and often without any sense of disloyalty. They even assemble in groups to influence the offer and get the best price or contract terms. The New Consumer demands a different kind of customer relationship, one that warrants an entirely different approach to strategic consumer marketing.

SUMMARY POINTS

- Consumption today is about the satisfaction of consumer wants and desires rather than the fulfilment of consumer needs.

- The process of consumption is widely recognized as a management issue, rather than simply a market phenomenon.

- The starting point for managing the consumption process should be the consumer, not the product, and marketing strategy needs to reflect this.

- New Consumers are exercised by time, lead complex lives, seek experiences, are marketing literate and highly demanding, and are IT enabled. This creates a different set of expectations to be met in the new marketplace.

- The New Consumer represents unprecedented challenges for marketers.

- Rethinking the consumer means rethinking marketing.
- The traditional command-and-control approach to consumption management must be replaced by more collaborative methods that involve and value the consumer.

Concerns of Brand Owners and Retailers   3

The challenge for brand owners and retailers is 'innovate or die'.

While many consumer brand owners recognize the symptoms of revolutionary change within the marketing environment, few have been able to interpret and respond to them meaningfully because of seemingly more pressing business demands. Among these immediate issues is the need to address concerns about the manufacturer–retailer relationship. Consolidation within the retail sector is continuing to increase the downward pressure on price, making it difficult for manufacturers to manoeuvre in terms of market position. Added to this, the impact of globalization has placed the future of manufacturing in question. Over recent years, the focus of producers and retailers has been supply chain management. However, for many organizations, simply improving efficiencies is no longer enough to achieve sustainability. Today's key business imperative is to balance cost reduction and sales growth.

Retailers are facing major challenges. Retail spending as a proportion of gross domestic product (GDP) has fallen significantly over the past couple of decades. This disturbing trend and the emergence of the New Consumer are forcing retailers to abandon their 'one size fits all' approach and to focus instead on managing consumer heterogeneity through marketing strategies resulting in narrower and deeper retail concepts.

KEY ISSUES FOR BRAND OWNERS

Research into the key business issues concerning fmcg brand owners by consultants Cap Gemini Ernst & Young[1] in 2001 underlined the overriding challenge of dealing with change in the competitive environment. Four main concerns were identified: the force of globalization, debate about the future of manufacturing, the growth in retailer power, and the need to manage the balance between cutting costs and growing sales.

The Force of Globalization

Organizational profitability and growth are the key drivers of a marketing strategy that has at its core the standardization of business structures, products and processes along global (or at least regional) lines. For many global brand manufacturers, a policy of standardization means adopting the philosophy that investments in product development and promotions provide greater returns if they are not limited to a single national market. The internationalization or globalization of business activity can lead to the de-duplication of roles and factories across several countries, serving to make the organization leaner. For consumers, the first visible sign of such a strategy in operation is often the subtle name change of a well-known product. In the UK, for example, Jif became Cif (see Figure 3.1), Oil of Ulay became Oil of Olay and Marathon became Snickers.

Production-driven, supply-chain thinking usually dominates a globalization strategy as producers seek to rationalize their number of stock-keeping units (SKUs) so as to avoid adding complexity to the supply chain. Several fmcg companies worldwide are involved in programmes that will severely reduce the number of SKUs they have to support. Unilever, for example, is currently amputating its long tail of under-performing brands, a process that will leave it with 400 strong-growth 'power brands', as compared to the heavily diluted pool of 1,600 it started with.

The main problem with a strategy of standardization is that it seldom acknowledges the consumption-led economy. Consumers themselves are not standard; they differ from one market to another. Fmcg giants risk alienation by offering a 'one size fits all' product range. Coca-Cola recognized this when it abandoned the mantra 'think global, act local' in favour of 'think local, act local'. The company wisely decided that manufacturing operations should be embedded in the local culture.

Global brand owners also have to deal with the fact that in some national markets, brands can remain strong and profitable even though they may never become international players. This can create conflict between local and global management over whether or not the brand in question should

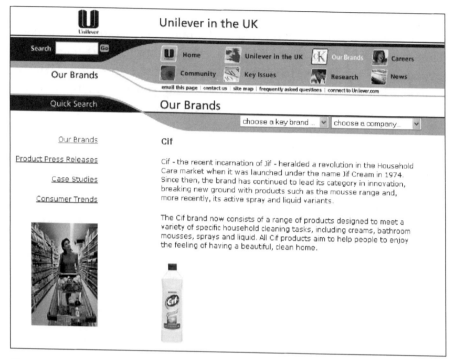

Figure 3.1 Jif changed to Cif as a result of globalization
Reproduced by permission of Unilever

be retained within the global portfolio. Success in managing a global portfolio is, therefore, marked by finding the right balance between standardization and customization.

The Debate about the Future of Manufacturing

In order to deal with the increasingly competitive environment and respond effectively to shareholder demands, fmcg companies have been forced to take a long, hard look at their businesses. Many are questioning the value brought to their company and brands by retaining ownership of the actual manufacturing process, and are evaluating outsourcing as a serious proposition. That this debate is taking place at all signifies a radical change in thinking for fmcg manufacturers, who have long regarded the manufacturing process as something of a sacred cow.

Nike, Ericsson and Sara Lee are among those brand owners providing indications of a possible way forward. Nike, for example, famously sees itself as a provider of lifestyles, conveyed through sportswear innovation, design and styling. It has never regarded production as a core competence. The manufacturing strategy implied by Nike's approach is one focused on coordinating access to external resources and ensuring effective collaboration between internal functions and contract manufacturers, particularly in the areas of new product development. The management of these crucial relationships is therefore key.

In taking the decision to follow a manufacturing strategy of 'innovate and coordinate', rather than 'own and operate', the brand owner is making product innovation and development a core competence and is focusing on the areas that drive growth and shareholder value. Use of such a strategy among fmcg manufacturers also demonstrates that they no longer see themselves as product companies and are repositioning themselves as service companies with a product offering. This move resonates with the economic trend away from a pure manufacturing base to an over-whelmingly services oriented economy. Those brand owners treading boldly into this new realm are effectively launching themselves into a new way of thinking to ensure their survival.

The Growth in Retailer Power

Brand owners are increasingly feeling the threat posed by industry consolidation, as the balance of power is tipped in favour of savvy retailers. It is becoming commonplace for retailers to use their intermediate position to negotiate prices, trade terms, shorter delivery times and tailored promotions, securing a win–win situation for themselves and their customers. They are also managing to persuade manufacturers to enter into vendor-managed inventory agreements, where the supplier actively manages the customer's inventory. The fear factor is intensifying in the UK amid speculation about whether Asda/Wal-Mart are planning further acquisitions that would bring them head-to-head with Tesco, Britain's biggest supermarket chain. Wal-Mart is the world's biggest retailer with annual sales of more than £140 billion. It possesses massive purchasing power and can buy goods very cheaply from Asia and developing nations.

Further stress in the manufacturer–retailer relationship stems from the pressure to standardize pricing and trade terms (following the introduction of the Euro), the competitive threat of high-quality own-label products, and the shrinking shelf space available for brands. When retailer–supplier negotiations come down to pure muscle power, the retailers have the edge simply because the fmcg sector is more fragmented. Manufacturers have tried to improve their position by maximizing the power of their 'must stock' brands, but very few of these represent brands that retailers would genuinely fear losing.

In some cases a more collaborative relationship is developing where the manufacturer recognizes that the retailer incurs an opportunity cost (of not achieving maximum potential sales), and works with the retailer to address this by supplying not just products but also value-added services that support the products. The key to such cooperation is the mutual sharing of information. Private web-based exchanges, which require the integration of both internal systems, are often used to share data and ideas. In this way, Nestlé improved its on-shelf availability in Sainsbury's stores to 97% while its overstocking fell by 25%.

The Need to Balance Cost Reduction and Sales Growth

Brand owners, especially food manufacturers, are under increasing pressure from the large retail multiples to reduce their trade prices and increase their service levels. In response, manufacturers are trying to eliminate wastage and excess costs from all corners of their cost base. At the same time, they are trying to find additional sales volumes to meet analysts' sales forecasts and shareholders' expected return on investment. So how well are they managing the balance between cutting costs and growing sales?

Unilever's strategy is typical. The company plans to eliminate 100 of its 380 manufacturing sites as part of its well-publicized 'Path to Growth' initiative. It is targeting top-line growth of 5–6% by 2004 through its focus on cost reduction and brand rationalization. However, cost reduction programmes come at a price: €6 billion of restructuring costs in Unilever's case. Unilever chairman Niall Fitzgerald is confident the targeted savings of €1.5 billion, together with purchasing savings of the same magnitude, will finance the company's ambitious growth plans.

The growth strategies of major fmcg companies all share an emphasis on cost reduction and service improvement. Achieving competitive advantage is becoming harder as both quality and cost-efficient production are no longer distinguishing factors in the marketplace. For decades now, most manufacturers have been addressing the issue of resource wastage and few would stand out as *in*efficient. The proportion of savings that they can generate for reinvestment in growth therefore depends on the effectiveness with which they implement their respective cost reduction programmes. Taking cost out of a business has historically been a more traumatic – but also a more predictable – fiscal strategy than trying to grow revenues. And while corporate acquisition can offer significant scope for investment capital, most would agree that innovation and organic growth represent more prudent options.

The Search for Innovation

All of these issues, combined with low inflation and price transparency throughout Europe, mean there is no end in sight to the price debate for manufacturers. Low-cost production and distribution become the minimum requirements for staying in the game. Achieving a step change in performance requires a radical solution, and it is focused innovation that offers the most promising source of organic growth. There should be innovation in the relationship between manufacturer and retailer and in the creation of the next wave of products and services. The solution lies in adaptability: that is, the ability to concentrate on short product cycles and product innovation based on profound insight into the value consumers are seeking. For consumer marketers this means having a value-centric orientation in the business and a way of managing that enables innovation.

THE RETAILERS' RESPONSE[2]

While many brand owners see retailers as the cause of their key business concerns, retailers themselves face daunting challenges. First and foremost among these is a long-term pattern of declining spend. In 1980, the retail sector represented 46.6% of GDP. Today, that figure has roughly halved. This is because most consumers have everything they need and retail expenditure is essentially concentrated on 'non-essentials', in satisfying their wants and desires. As a result, retailers compete with an ever-expanding range of competitors, encompassing such areas of expenditure as holidays, eating out and personal luxuries.

A closer look at this trend shows variations across different types of business. In food retail, this trend is typical of developed economies, as there is a limit to how much people can eat and eating out of home has become increasingly popular. This is why the grocery retailers are so keen to develop their non-food businesses. In clothing retail, there has been a loss of share since the late 1990s, probably driven more by a lack of excitement in the product offers than anything else. In contrast, the home improvement retail business has been a success story: sales in do-it-yourself (DIY) and electrical products, and furniture and soft furnishings have shown significant growth.

Retailers are also facing challenges in respect to business location. In the UK, there has been an escalation in out-of-town shopping, forcing many traditional high-street retailers out of business. Non-central sites carry lower rents and opportunities for larger stores, making for a more attractive proposition. At the same time, the cost of siting businesses in towns and cities is rising for two important reasons: the introduction of inflexible, upwards only, rental arrangements; and the rapid expansion of fast-food outlets, coffee shops and mobile phone retailers.

However, this current trend is likely to be reversed with the property industry's proposed introduction of a code of practice that will enable retailers to negotiate more favourable rental agreements and the natural effects of market saturation. Furthermore, out-of-town rents are being driven upwards by buoyant demand for DIY and electrical goods as well as new interest from clothing retailers.

In store, price is still a significant issue for retailers. Continuation in the use of 'every day low pricing' (EDLP) and promotions to leverage consumer interest and revenue/profit is being questioned as consumer expectations heighten and additional demands are placed on finite resources. So, caught under mounting pressure from intensifying competition and 'margin squeeze', what should the retailer's strategy for survival be? Several options exist, and these may be used in isolation or combination.

Trading across Multiple Locations

In the UK, the rule of thumb for selecting the right sales location used to be that if you could see McDonald's out of one eye and Marks & Spencer out of the other, somewhere in the middle was probably just right. It is no longer that simple, as location and store format have become linked to segmentation strategy. The major multiples, for example, are increasingly tapping the potential of smaller, convenience and food-to-go stores in neighbourhood and suburban locations. In 2002, Tesco acquired the convenience store chains One Stop and Nite-and-Day, with the intention of rebranding them to increase the number of Tesco Express outlets from 100 to more than 500.

Trading across Multiple Formats

Major retailers across a range of industries no longer confine themselves to single-store formats but have developed a number of approaches to maximize trading opportunities. Larger store formats are becoming more common for retailing groceries, clothing, DIY and electrical goods. Among smaller format stores, retail growth is expected to come from new builds (mainly grocery), concession units (electricals and furniture) and store 'implants', such as the Health & Beauty which Boots is trialling as an 'implant' in Sainsbury's supermarkets.

Use of Multiple Channels

With the rapid take-up of new technologies, retailers are utilizing an ever-expanding mix of channels. For example, Next is one of a number of companies to offer its goods across a range of channels: online, mail and telephone ordering services are available to its customers. Overall, the nature of the online offer will probably continue to differ across the range of product categories. For example, it is transactional in nature in clothing, grocery and electricals, and more focused on promotion and the provision of information to consumers in the areas of DIY, furniture, and health and beauty. Despite the hype surrounding e-commerce, experts predict that by 2005 little more than 5% of retail sales will be online. The majority of these purchases will be made by consumers in the 26–45-year-old age bracket and the over 50s, or 'silver surfers'.

Editing Choice in Store

The attention of retail managers is increasingly focusing on how consumers find their way around product ranges within stores, as well as how they navigate store aisles. New Consumers are looking for 'edited choice'; that is, visible guidelines to help them save time and effort. Smart retailers who understand this particular consumer want are targeting specific groupings of products to appeal to specific segments of New Consumers. For example, a range of specialist additive-free products will be grouped together within a supermarket, rather than following the traditional practice of locating additive-free biscuits with other biscuits and additive-free bread with other breads.

Enhancing Retail Branding

Retailers are developing their brands by creating new retail brand identities targeted at particular market segments. A retail brand such as The Link, a new Dixons Group brand, works best in heterogeneous markets where economies of scale are of limited significance. In contrast, retail brand extensions are more commonly used where the core retail brand has built up a strong level of consumer equity, such as the strategy Boots is pursuing with its Boots Opticians brand.

Developing Multinational Operations

Taking retail concepts overseas is a seductive proposition but few retailers have made a success of it. Failed attempts to recreate business success in other countries usually result from a lack of understanding and appreciation of the way that markets operate. There may be crucial differences in the way property is owned and managed, or how employers and employees interact. Sometimes it is a simple misreading of local consumer needs. However, some retailers do manage to succeed in establishing multinational operations, and certain markets have become the focus of highly competitive activity. Tesco and Wal-Mart, for instance, are both aggressively expanding in central Europe and the Asia Pacific region.

Pursuing Customer Loyalty

Customer loyalty represents the Holy Grail for retailers, who now have the potential to use consumer data to build powerful, knowledge-based

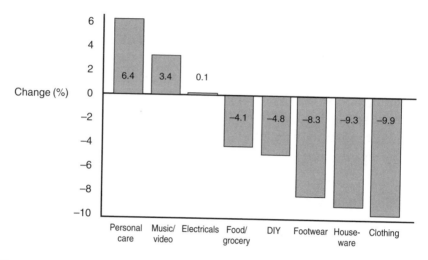

Figure 3.2 The decline in loyalty, 1999–2002. Adapted from Verdict, 2002
Reproduced by permission of World Advertising Research Centre

consumer relationships. However, as market analyst Verdict concludes, consumer loyalty is eroding across most sectors. Consumer churn is growing most strongly in the areas of clothing, housewares and footwear, followed by DIY and food. Figure 3.2 illustrates this decline in loyalty (the change in the average number of people saying they were loyal to one retailer). In order to arrest this trend, retailers have introduced a variety of loyalty schemes and programmes. In the UK, current benchmarks have been set by Tesco and Boots, whose Clubcard and Advantage Card, respectively, are carried by a majority of consumers.

The launch of Nectar, a 'next-generation' loyalty scheme backed by Sainsbury's, BP, Debenhams and Barclaycard, introduced in 2002, invigorated the battle for consumer loyalty (see Table 3.1). Nectar's rewards offer focuses on frequently consumed 'low ticket' items. Loyalty points may be redeemed by founding partners, Sainsbury's and Argos, or by alliance partners, McDonald's, Blockbuster, Legoland and Odeon Cinemas.

Critics of these loyalty schemes argue that what is being created is a 'loyalty currency', rather than any genuine sense of affiliation with and support for a particular retailer. They claim that successful loyalty schemes only work because retailers are able to take consumer information and turn it into actions, which in turn provide the consumer with recognizable benefits. These benefits strengthen the consumer's bond with the company

Table 3.1 The battle of the loyalty cards (at Nectar's launch)

	Nectar	Tesco Clubcard	British Airways Airmiles	Boots Advantage
Number of members	1 million	10 million	6 million	13 million
How points are earned	2 points for each £1 spent at Sainsbury's and Debenhams; 1 point for each litre of BP fuel or £2 spent on a Barclaycard	1 point for every £1 spent in Tesco stores and other participating outlets	1 Air Mile for every £5 spent on flights, 15 litres of Shell fuel or £20 spent on a NatWest, Coutts or Ulster Bank credit card	4 points for every £1 spent on Boots products; 1 point per £1 spent on Boots services, e.g. opticians
Where can points be exchanged?	40 outlets	150 outlets	n/a	Boots stores
What could be obtained for an annual spend of £8,400?	18 meals at McDonalds/ 3 child admissions to Legoland/1 return flight to Brussels	40 video rentals from Blockbuster/8 adult admissions to Legoland/ 5 return flights to Paris	3 return flights to Amsterdam/4 adult and 4 child admissions to Legoland/1 return flight to Barcelona	12 no.7 make-up collections/8 cut and blow dry sessions at Toni & Guy/1 course of tooth whitening treatment

Source: The Times, London, 21 September 2002 – NI Syndication, London, 21 September 2002

because the consumer can see that the company cares about them enough to reward their business. However, a scheme that simply rewards the consumer but fails to capture in a meaningful way the vital flow of information from consumer transactions is a sales promotion scheme, however large it might be.

IMPLICATIONS FOR CONSUMER MARKETING

The mass markets of the production-driven economy have given way to the diverse, demanding markets of the consumption-led economy. In response, brand owners and retailers are replacing their 'one size fits all' consumer marketing strategies with ones that are more customized and personalized. The era of maximizing scale is over and the future of retailing looks to be about creating retail concepts that appeal to smaller clusters of consumers. While certain 'category killers' (giant out-of-town superstore brands that focus on retailing a single category of products, such as B&Q in DIY) will survive as they currently stand, most retailers are taking radical action. They are creating a 'narrower and deeper' type of offer in the hope of gaining a higher penetration of consumer spend. Micro-retailing, where retailers make a limited range of products available in a small store to a highly targeted audience, can only be successful if it is based on meaningful insights into the value being sought by the New Consumer. Of course, this presupposes that a value-centric orientation exists within the business.

SUMMARY POINTS

* Both brand owners and retailers need to adopt a value-centric orientation and an approach to marketing that enables adaptability, creativity and innovation.

* The impact of globalization and questions surrounding manufacturing, cost-effectiveness and competition are causing brand owners to rationalize their portfolios.

* There is no end in sight to the trade price issue as retailers consolidate and continue to exert downward pressure on prices.

* To achieve improvements in brand performance, brand owners must deliver consumer-focused innovation.

- Faced with a declining share of GDP and lower levels of consumer loyalty, retailers are increasingly adopting multi-location, multi-format, multi-channel and multinational strategies.
- Micro-retailing is creating narrower and deeper retail offerings.

New Consumer Marketing 4

New Consumer Marketing champions a new and viable way of marketing.

New Consumer Marketing (NCM) does not just advocate a new focus for marketing; it champions a new way of doing marketing. It breaks away from the mechanistic models of the production-driven era and provides fresh thinking on managing new patterns of consumer growth. It focuses on the demand side of business, taking the consumer as its starting point, not its final destination. As a concept, NCM combines the strengths of an organization's people and processes, and enables marketers to break out of the binary thinking that has seen businesses swing between a singular emphasis on process or on people.

NCM is at an early stage of development. Its evolution as a specific management discipline is being influenced by an eclectic body of individuals who recognize that new marketing approaches and attitudes are needed. Most established marketing thinking has grown out of the mechanistic age of marketing, where the certainties of mass markets provided a sense of security for brand owners and retailers. The present marketing environment is no longer as static and certain as it used to be, and there is a growing need to find more appropriate marketing tools and techniques to connect better with consumers.

NEW CONSUMER MARKETING – WHAT IS IT?

New Consumer Marketing is not simply another way of managing the marketing mix. It is an emerging business discipline that addresses a range of issues relevant to competing successfully in a particular market. Its key objective is to establish sustainable competitive advantage through superior processes of value definition, value creation and value delivery. At the heart of each of these processes is a core capability – insight, innovation and agility. These capabilities enable the organization to develop consumer responsiveness; that is, to deliver the value required by its consumer segments cost-effectively.

NCM helps marketers make sense of the complexity and apparent chaos that defines today's consumer markets. In this post-quake economy, managers find themselves searching for frameworks and tools that will enable them to master very different market conditions. NCM provides fresh thinking on where and how to focus marketing attention and resources in this consumption-led economy. It is a response by leading-edge marketers to the outstanding challenges posed by the New Consumer, whose arrival is marked by heightened competition, technological developments that have created an interactive marketplace and increasingly irrelevant consumption management practice that is struggling to succeed through Relationship Marketing (RM) and Customer Relationship Management (CRM).

A Response to the New Consumer

Consumers today are faced with overwhelming choice. For the most part, their needs are taken care of and their discretionary expenditure is focused on satisfying their wants and desires. As discussed in Chapter 2, New Consumers' expectations of products, services and brands extend beyond 'features' and 'benefits' to 'experiences'. Even with this insight, brand owners and retailers face an uphill struggle in connecting with consumers. Their brand messages compete for the attention of an increasingly sophisticated audience, who are bombarded with information from rival sources. As author Seth Godin (1999) has noted, a wealth of data becomes a poverty of attention.

Furthermore, it is harder to reach consumers who live highly fragmented lives and display multiple personalities, and who change suppliers at the click of button. Such sophisticated and demanding consumers are not confined to a static marketplace but roam freely within an interactive one. New routes to market emerge all the time, making it easier for consumers to go to market. They can research products and make their purchases offline or online, or both, as is their preference. For the consumer, controlling the relationship in this interactive marketplace extends to controlling the value proposition more directly and forcefully than ever before. For instance, the web can easily support build-to-order manufacturing, where consumers specify the colour, size or configuration of a product they want.

A Response to the Interactive Marketplace

Developments in IT bring with them both opportunities and threats. For example, as we move from a state of interaction into an age of integration, consumers will increasingly have access to information on the move and the ability to demand faster, better and cheaper service. At the same time, mobile commerce makes it possible for marketers to communicate more effectively with consumers: marketing messages can be targeted and consistent, and consumer feedback can be received and assimilated.

For the consumer, the costs of doing business are likely to fall as IT offers an opportunity to find the best value for money offers. For example, www.carsurvey.org and www.moneysupermarket.com enable consumers to make comparisons at the click of a mouse, while other websites bring individual consumers together, empowering them to use their collective bargaining power. The next step on from this is the development of personal agents, or sites that coordinate and control the access of suppliers to meet an individual's specific requirements; for example, a domestic services agent that manages suppliers of utilities, groceries, mortgage and banking services, etc.

The Internet opens up business transparency and effectively transfers the power in the relationship to consumers. Economists suggest that, under these conditions, firms will end up as price takers in a near perfect market (markets in which conditions of free and open competition more or less exist). The so-called 'rate tart' – the informed, confident consumer who switches between companies to gain the benefit of the best financial deals on offer – is already a reality for suppliers of personal financial services. In the music industry consumers have taken control of both production and consumption. Music lovers have exploited the advantages of MP3, a standard file format that enables digital music files to be compressed so they can be downloaded via the Internet in a reasonable time and without losing too much audio quality. Consumers can e-copy songs and entire audio CDs without having to pay for the music (an opportunity for musical artists to flaunt their talent; a threat to the music industry in lost income).

A significant effect of the pace of change in IT has been the emergence of time as a competitive dimension. Organizations find themselves having to operate in 'Martini mode', or – in the words of the drink's advert – 'any time, any place, any where'. The term '24/7' has entered the English language, superseding the earlier phrase 'open all hours'. Competing on the basis of time demands a rapid response capability. Organizations need to develop business strategies that ensure adaptability. The turbulent marketplace means there is no certainty in long-term demand forecasts.

A Response to Ineffective Consumption Management

While the evolution of the consumer and IT were beginning to challenge the marketing *status quo*, marketing focus shifted from managing individual transactions to building consumer relationships. Relationship Marketing concentrated on retaining customers rather than acquiring them, simply because there were fewer 'new' customers left to acquire, competition was tougher, and the correlation between profitability and long-term customer relationships had been made.

As a framework, RM provided much useful learning about the benefits of focusing on retention and developing relationships over time with customers and other stakeholders. It introduced the idea that all of these relationships are interdependent, and it has encouraged managers to visualize the marketing space as a web, or network, of interconnected relationships based on mutual interests. However, RM falls short of enabling organizations to deal effectively with the New Consumer in the consumption-led economy that is characterized by a dynamic complexity.

In many organizations, developments in IT and computational technology were applied to the business of developing a CRM strategy. It is now widely accepted that the vast majority of expenditure on CRM systems has failed to meet expectations. This is because CRM is a poorly defined concept and there is little agreement on how to implement it. Recent research suggests that CRM should not be attempted by an organization unless there is congruence between its marketing strategy, IT strategy and corporate culture. The challenge for CRM systems is delivering value into consumer markets characterized by high levels of heterogeneity.

NCM implies that the challenges thrown up by changing cultures of consumption and an increasingly competitive environment can only be met through a step change in strategic thinking, which, in essence, means moving the consumer up the corporate agenda. The board's focus must switch from supply-chain management to managing the demand system, and that starts with the 4Cs (consumer needs and wants, cost, convenience and communication) rather than the 4Ps (price, product, place and promotion). Marketers, who manage the critical interface between the new marketplace and the organization, are best placed to bring about this change in focus. NCM therefore offers an opportunity to overcome a decade or so of debate about the contribution marketing makes to the success of a business by redefining marketing's role and status in a way that also sends it to new heights and into a new realm.

NEW CONSUMER MARKETING – WHAT DOES IT MEAN?

NCM means adopting a value-centric orientation in the organization and drawing on learning from the new science of complexity. In this way, marketing can be conceptualized as a business discipline that enables an organic approach, focused around key processes of value definition, creation and delivery, and one that combines an emphasis on people and process.

Adopting Value-Centricity

As the practice of marketing has evolved in response to market conditions, the underlying philosophy of a business in relation to the customers it serves has shifted (see Table 4.1). Transaction marketing was based on a sales orientation with the aim of acquiring as many new customers as possible. Profit was generated through increased sales volume. Relationship Marketing switched the emphasis to developing greater profitability through customer satisfaction, underpinned by a retention orientation. The realities of the consumption-led economy demand that the focus of a business shift again to insight, innovation and agility to achieve profitability, based on having a value-centric orientation in the business.

Table 4.1 The evolution of the marketing orientation

Focus	Means	End
Sales orientation	Transactional marketing	Profits through acquiring customers
Retention orientation	Relationship Marketing and CRM	Profits through customer satisfaction
Value orientation	Demand system management	Profits through insight, innovation, agility

Value-centricity generates revenue growth and improved profitability through a focus on the demand side of the business. It means moving beyond a relationship emphasis to one that has at its core the definition, creation and delivery of value. If an organization can meet the value expectations of the consumer, then a long-term and profitable relationship is more likely to follow. The key is having value as the starting point; otherwise the relationship development strategy (and the CRM tools perhaps used to deliver it) will not work as intended.

In NCM, value-centricity therefore replaces the focus on customer retention as the underlying orientation of a business. Profitability is generated through delivering the value consumers want to buy into and the organization wants to deliver: that is, *value on the consumer's terms*, as demanded and maybe even dictated by them. This value component marks the process of exchange that takes place between the consumer and the organization; it is the 'thing' that the consumer gets in return for what they give. Organizations must learn how to operate in this consumer 'space'.

In order to meet New Consumers' expectations, organizations need to fine-tune their understanding of the factors that create this value, those that maintain it and, equally, those that destroy it. Understanding the nature of the different value factors is also an opportunity to review the 'phantoms' that exist in every organization; that is, those features of a brand that the organization believes add value but which are not rated at all by consumers. These are the 'taken for granted' elements that can be eliminated from the process, resulting in cost savings for the organization.

Applying Science

Organizational understanding of the make-up of value consumers are seeking has to be continuously updated. This is because the new marketplace is *dynamically* complex. The Internet is perhaps the most striking example of this. Experts believe that the speed, scope and scale of market change will be driven by two laws relating to technology. The first was described by Intel founder Gordon Moore, who declared that every 18 months chip density (and therefore computing power) would double while costs would remain unchanged. The second law is attributed to Robert Metcalfe, the founder of 3Com Corporation and inventor of Ethernet. What he describes as the experienced utility of belonging to an electronic network increases exponentially with the number of users. In other words, the more who join a network, the more sense it makes for others to do the same. Those who choose not to join miss out in more ways than one. Meeting the challenges posed by cheaper computing power and an emphasis on networks are expected to characterize future developments in consumer marketing strategy.

To make a value-centric orientation a reality in this new marketplace requires a shift in mindset about the way an organization is capable of functioning. It means moving from thinking linearly and mechanistically, to thinking organically, as this holds the key to consumer responsiveness. Living entities are more capable of adaptability, the key requirement for survival in the new marketplace. Marketing needs to adjust to these new realities and become a systemic, holistic and, above all, dynamically complex activity.

This view connects with the new science of complexity in which interaction is characterized as a near chaotic state. Complexity science is about searching for patterns among an abundance of seemingly random phenomena in the universe and about establishing how order emerges from the apparent chaos. To use an example, down in the garden pond in spring, a mass of froglets experiencing the growth of new legs and the disappearance of a tail will emerge from the water in a cacophony of sound and hop haphazardly on to dry land. To an observer this may appear a chaotic scene but the froglets are actually only demonstrating complex adaptive system behaviour, based on principles of self-organization.

Complexity science is aptly named and has spawned two major sub-strands of research: chaos theory and complex adaptive systems (Gleick, 1987; Pascale, 1990). It was advances in computational technology in the 1960s that made the science possible, led by the work of Edward Lorenz on chaos theory. His contribution is based on research into weather systems and left the idea that 'small changes can produce large results' in the popular mind. Edification in this field came later in James Gleick's 1987 best-seller, *Chaos: Making a New Science*, although these ideas were not transferred to the business arena. The behaviour of complex adaptive systems, however, offers more scope for parallels with the world of commerce. These systems are found everywhere and comprise independent but dynamically interacting agents that develop their optimum performance by continually learning, changing and adapting to their environments. However chaotic the process looks at any point, it always evolves to a state of creative order, one famously described by Norman Packard as the 'edge of chaos'.

The appeal of complexity science to business theorists is that it provides a way of thinking about how the underlying processes and relationships in a company can be organized to enable the company to become as adaptive and creative as possible in the face of continual change. This convergence of science and business provides a rich seam to be mined. And Richard Pascale, in his 1990 book *Managing on the Edge*, is credited with leading the way here although other authors also advocate this emerging biological thesis. Champions of this scientific analogy are not, however, suggesting that commerce will start behaving as nature does but instead believe that it can be helpful in finding a different way of looking at business issues. Business may be able to learn how to understand complexity and find a way of responding dynamically to change.

Breaking out of Binary Thinking

NCM emerges at the confluence of these two streams of thinking – the new science of complexity and the evolving discipline of marketing. NCM is, therefore, different from the prevailing marketing paradigm. It is a business discipline that enables the organization to master the increasingly dynamic and complex process of going to market in a systemic and holistic way. It provides managers with a means of identifying and mobilizing people and processes to help them become as adaptive and creative as possible against the background of a complex marketing environment.

A systemic approach to managing the dynamic complexity of the new marketplace enables organizations to break out of the binary thinking that has seen businesses swing between a singular emphasis on process or on people. Marketing thinking has been heavily influenced by the mechanistic models that emerged in the era of the production-driven economy. These reductionist approaches are epitomized by the 1936 silent movie *Modern Times*, starring Charlie Chaplin. Behind the slapstick and the sentiment in this film, the little tramp finds himself at odds with society and fights to hold onto the remnants of his tattered dignity and individuality. It is a pointed spoof of the dehumanization of man in an industrialized society. It derides mechanization as we see Charlie on the assembly line tightening nuts at breakneck speed – the perfect cog in a wheel of misfortune. Eventually, a nervous breakdown forces him to leave the factory but he cannot stop tightening nuts even when there are none to tighten.

Frederick Taylor and his book *The Principles of Scientific Management* are most closely associated with these approaches to management (Taylor, 1967). His ideas influenced generations of business theorists, from Henry Ford and his mass production of the Model T-Ford automobile through to advocates of more recent marketing trends (including the quality movement, benchmarking, BPR, McDonaldization and lean production), right up to the current flirtation with Six Sigma (an approach that focuses on minimizing production errors). At the heart of these developments is a belief that there is only one right way to complete a task and that a business should be driven by efficiency based on the standardization of processes.

In between these emphases on process, the management pendulum has swung back to a stress on people to achieve business success. In the 1950s, Douglas McGregor identified two contrasting styles of management, command-and-control and self-management, which he termed Theory X and Theory Y (McGregor, 1960). He advocated a more participative approach and influenced many theorists who followed him, among them Charles Handy (1989, 1994, 1997). These humanist approaches to management found their expression in the concept of empowerment. Volvo was among the first to implement them, replacing individual car workers with teams of workers who were given decision-making roles in the business. This must have been enough of a change to make Henry Ford turn in his grave.

NCM encourages the synergy of both 'people' and 'process' combined by taking a systemic and holistic approach to marketing. This way of thinking offers an opportunity to identify the key underlying processes and relationships that help an organization function organically, enabling it to adapt, create and respond appropriately to the changing marketing environment.

NEW CONSUMER MARKETING – WHO IS INVOLVED?

New Consumer Marketing has come about as result of the thinking of an eclectic body of managers, consultants and academics. These individuals are drawn from a number of different spheres. These spheres include the development of networks and network thinking, where Tim Berners-Lee, inventor of the World Wide Web, Bill Gates, whose company Microsoft touches all our lives, Nicholas Negroponte, founder-director of MIT's Media Lab, Don Tapscott, management consultant, and John Seely Brown, chief scientist at Xerox PARC, have made significant contributions (Berners-Lee and Fischetti, 1999; Gates and Hemingway, 1999; Negroponte, 1995; Tapscott, 1996, 1998; Tapscott et al., 2000; Brown and Duguid, 2000).

Other ideas have come from insights emanating from work that draws management closer to the world of the living sciences. Stanford professor Richard Pascale, for example, sets out to draw a new management model based on complex living systems in *Surfing the Edge of Chaos* (Pascale et al., 2000), while Arie de Geus, former head of planning at Shell, originated the concept of the learning organization and presents a gardener's organic view of managing business in *The Living Company* (Geus, 1999).

Two further strands of thought have come from academia where, first, work on interpreting contemporary consumer behaviour has thrown light on the New Consumer[1] and, second, there is a growing body of research and work that highlights value as the new key driver of strategy.[2]

Finally, there are managers and consultants who are simply doing it or preaching it, in some form or another. Many of these individuals and the companies they work for are mentioned, or become the focus of short case studies, in the following chapters. What starts to distinguish those practising NCM is that they share a common vision of a virtual compass giving direction as to how best to manage the process of marketing to New Consumers. Unlike a traditional compass where the needle always settles on due North, the New Consumer marketing compass uses 'value' as a reference point. This guides thinking in managing the processes of value definition, creation and delivery, ensuring that the organization produces the value that consumers want to buy into and the organization wants to deliver.

IMPLICATIONS FOR CONSUMER MARKETING

New Consumer Marketing has important implications for *consumer marketing*. It introduces a new approach and a new way of doing it. NCM goes beyond the management of the marketing mix and concerns itself with major business issues relating to the organization's positioning in the marketplace and the consumers it seeks to serve, determining how and where it competes. These issues are of a company-wide and high-level nature that will impact the business in the long run. How well an organization masters NCM has significant consequences for its future profitability. Mastery of NCM is dependent on having a framework in place to enable the organization to describe and position its marketing strategy. This is considered in Chapter 5.

SUMMARY POINTS

- New Consumer Marketing (NCM) is a response to the arrival of the New Consumer, the development of the interactive marketplace and ineffective consumption management.

- NCM is a business discipline whose key objective is creating sustainable competitive advantage through superior processes of value definition, value creation and value delivery. It demands a change in strategic thinking that moves the consumer up the corporate agenda.

- NCM draws on thinking from the new science of complexity. Organizations need to develop adaptability to survive in the new dynamic marketplace. The key is achieving consumer responsiveness through insight, innovation and organizational agility.

- NCM means rethinking marketing as a living demand system that has at its core a value-centric orientation.

- Value is defined as *value on the consumer's terms*; it is the 'thing' that consumers get in return for what they give. Brand owners and retailers must learn how to operate in this customer 'space'.

A Model of New Consumer Marketing 5

A New Consumer Marketing model conceptualizes New Consumer Marketing practice.

No management learning is complete without the development of a model or two. Models help in conveying complex ideas, but are more than simple visual aids. Business models normally fall into one of two types: operational or conceptual. Operational business models offer a way of linking inputs and outputs within the managerial context to improve performance based on empirical evidence. Conceptual business models, on the other hand, precede this stage of development and assist in making sense of a large body of scholarly knowledge and management insight. The New Consumer Marketing model presented in this book is of the conceptual type. It represents a collection of assertions that identify important variables, and specifies how they are interrelated and why. As such, it provides a useful tool for marketers to formulate the way forward.

TO RECAP ...

Chapter 1 established that businesses today are operating in a time of radical transition: the certainties of the production-driven economy have been replaced by the uncertainties of the consumption-led economy. Consumption and the servicing of consumption now form the central motor of contemporary society. The tools and techniques of marketing, developed mainly in the production-driven era, are no longer applicable in the marketplace of the New Consumer. Furthermore, marketing's contribution to business is unclear.

Relationship Marketing (RM) was a strategic response by producers who found themselves operating in mature markets where greater profitability was shown to come from developing long-term relationships with customers. RM theory shifted marketing focus from customer acquisition to customer retention. While RM usefully highlighted the importance of building relationships with customers, consumers and other stakeholders, it fell short of enabling organizations to deal effectively with the New Consumer in a consumption-led economy. The implementation of RM strategies through CRM systems has also failed to meet expectations, leaving many marketers and non-marketers unclear about whether they should be focusing on people or process.

Chapter 2 showed that consumption management today is about the satisfaction of consumers' wants and desires, rather than solely the fulfilment of their needs. A wide range of organizations is recognizing that consumers, not products, drive the process of consumption and therefore the consumer should be the starting point for developing strategies to manage consumption. In other words, consumer marketers should base their activities on the 4Cs, rather than the 4Ps.

The chapter also introduced New Consumers' characteristic attitudes to time, their fragmented lifestyles and their motivating desire for experiences. New Consumers challenge current marketing thinking and practice because they are marketing literate, highly demanding and IT enabled. In effect, the 'make–sell' model of the old production-driven economy has given way to the 'tell–make' model of the new consumption-led economy. To succeed now and in the future, marketing strategy must actively address the heterogeneity of these empowered consumers.

Chapter 3 looked at the key concerns of brand owners and retailers, and found that, despite differences in the challenges they face, both are seeking similar solutions that focus on innovation. The impact of globalization is causing brand owners to rationalize their product portfolios and to question the wisdom of keeping manufacturing in-house. Should they 'own and operate' or 'innovate and coordinate'? Price is a key issue as retailers consolidate and continue to exert downward pressure on prices. Retailers, for their part, are suffering a decline in share of GDP, matched by a decline in consumer loyalty. They are increasingly choosing to trade across multiple locations, formats, channels and countries. Their partial solution to satisfying New Consumers – micro-retailing – is leading to the creation of narrower and deeper retail offerings.

In Chapter 4, New Consumer Marketing was positioned as a response to the challenges thrown up by changes in consumer culture and the wider competitive environment. It has emerged at the point where the evolution of consumer marketing meets with the new science of complexity. New Consumer Marketing places the consumer at the centre of the consumer marketing process and works to ensure that the consumer's perception of value is the yardstick of success. But this emergent business discipline differs from traditional marketing approaches in that it is about managing consumer demand in an organic manner, rather than managing consumer supply in a mechanistic fashion.

KEY CHALLENGES FACING NEW CONSUMER MARKETING

The key challenges facing consumer marketers have been thrown up by the tectonic change that has impacted the macro-marketing environment. In the shift from a production-driven to a consumption-led economy, conventional approaches to consumer marketing are not succeeding in enabling organizations to master the dynamic complexity of the new marketplace. These key challenges can be summarized as the need to:

- address the concerns of brand owners and retailers;
- embrace the New Consumer;
- help organizations develop real consumer responsiveness;
- lift marketing out of its crisis.

Addressing the Concerns of Brand Owners and Retailers

Brand owners are facing a period of significant change as a result of changing consumer demand. This, combined with consolidation among their customer base, has put them under increased pressure to satisfy these changing needs. While they would like to be focusing resources on innovation and new product development, instead they have no choice but to ruthlessly attack their cost base in order to meet retailers' price demands. Low-cost production and distribution become the minimum requirements for meeting these demands and staying in the game; competitive advantage is found elsewhere.

Retailers face their own challenges, driven by the declining proportion of GDP now attributed to retail spending. As the consumer base becomes more autonomous and diverse, the 'one size fits all' approach to developing retail concepts is no longer appropriate. Both brand owners and retailers are looking to enrich and expand the strategic options open to them. They need to adopt a value-centric orientation and an approach to marketing that enables adaptability and creativity. This will empower manufacturers to manoeuvre within the relationship and work towards delivering demand-led profit growth, while for retailers, it will enable them to profitably master the point of confluence where societal and economic changes and changes in consumer culture are being played out.

Embracing the New Consumer

What is clear is that there is an urgent need for fresh thinking in consumer marketing, to find different ways of managing the realities of the new marketplace. The management of consumption, now the driving force in the economy, needs to be rethought in light of the New Consumer. Sophisticated and demanding, at large in an interactive rather than a static marketplace, the New Consumer creates new challenges for organizations, which find the conventional tools of strategy making and tactical solutions developed in the mechanistic age of marketing of little help.

Success or failure will ultimately depend on their abilities to understand consumer behaviour in a time of continuous economic, social and technological change and, at the same time, to manage the organization's response. However, developing understanding is becoming more difficult as the approach of the production-driven era, which characterized consumers by using basic demographics, no longer gets us close enough to really comprehending buying motivations. The predictive power of these traditional categories has been eroded, and segmentation analyses that break buyers into simple caricatures of five or six types for entire markets often create more barriers to effectively connecting with them than they facilitate.

Developing Real Consumer Responsiveness

Growth is a business imperative. Organizations have learned that they 'cannot shrink their way to greatness'. Gary Hamel and C.K. Prahalad, in their book *Competing for the Future* (1994), came up with the term 'corporate anorexia' to describe the state many organizations found themselves in after the accountants had seized on concepts such as Business Process Re-engineering (BPR) and lean production (known as 'leanness'[1]), and introduced rationalization and downsizing programmes which left little to invest in new growth. An internally focused, cost-cutting strategy delivers short-term gains but does not address the issue of long-term growth. Breaking out of the cost-cutting cycle requires a more far-reaching strategy that anticipates the broader issues that will influence future performance.

Growth comes from the demand side of the business, which means doing the same thing better or doing something new. To achieve this, organizations need to connect better with consumers; they need to understand how to deliver the value that consumers are seeking in a continually adaptive and creative way. For many, supply-chain management has been the name of the game over recent years. However, in contrast to supply-chain thinking, New Consumer Marketing takes the consumer as the point of departure for the organization, not the final destination. In effect, the 'pipeline' is reversed and organizations become forced to see the delivery, creation and definition of their offering from the consumer's point of view. New Consumer Marketing goes beyond simply renaming this 'demand chain management' by advocating drawing on learning from the new sciences and conceptualizing marketing as a demand *system*.

Lifting Marketing Out of its Crisis

Criticism about the lack of clarity surrounding marketing's contribution to a business has been a feature of reports and articles over recent years. This is, in part, driven by the difficulties surrounding the measurement of marketing effectiveness but also by the fact that marketing is both equated with business unit strategy and located within the marketing mix. Without a clear emphasis as to its role, marketing languishes in a 'no man's land' and is badly placed to provide strategic leadership.

THE NEW CONSUMER MARKETING MODEL

The NCM model recognizes and tackles – on a conceptual level – these outstanding challenges. It advocates that organizations embrace the New

Consumer by adopting a value-centric orientation and refocus their structures on the three key processes of value definition, creation and delivery. These make up a demand system. The central component of a value-centric strategy is *value on the consumers' terms*, as demanded – maybe even dictated – by them. This value component marks the process of exchange that takes place between consumers and the organization; it is the 'thing' that consumers get in return for what they give.

A process is defined as an activity, or group of activities, that takes an input, adds value to it and provides an output to an internal or external customer. At the heart of each of these key processes is a core capability – insight, innovation and agility. These are the capabilities that enable brand owners and retailers to become adaptable and able to offer real consumer responsiveness.

Adopting a process approach entails a different way of working to that associated with traditional, vertical, hierarchical structures of functional departments. These static structures act as a barrier to performance. In focusing on processes, organizations take on a flatter, horizontal structure that enables them to be more responsive by speeding up decision-making processes and encouraging cross-functional collaboration, which helps maximize consumer value and operational cost-effectiveness. With an emphasis on understanding consumers and their value preferences, value-centric organizations draw key employees together in autonomous, multidisciplinary teams to focus resources around the main processes. Often these teams are temporary, enabling the organization to combine and recombine assets according to the nature of the opportunities that arise. These are firms that regard the organizational whole as greater than the sum of its parts. However, this does not mean that organizations cannot grow big. Tesco, for example, is one of a number of organizations that has succeeded in building the virtues of smallness into a large organization.

The NCM model adopts the principles of the new science to suggest an organic approach to consumer marketing. Where marketing is viewed as a systemic, holistic and dynamically complex activity, adaptability becomes an achievable goal. In business, systemic thinking offers a way of identifying the key underlying processes and relationships that help the organization to adapt, create and respond appropriately to the changing marketing environment. In this way, organizations are able to break out of the binary thinking that has long constrained management theory, and the model encourages the synergy of both 'people' and 'process' combined. In short, the static marketing function of the production-driven economy becomes a living demand system in the consumption-led economy.

The NCM model lifts marketing out of its crisis in terms of presenting a conceptual guide for practitioners for generating and managing the exchange process under conditions of competition. The NCM model provides a framework that enables an organization to describe and position its marketing strategy. In doing this, it identifies the consumer segments it seeks to serve, determining where and how it will compete. Working at the level of competitive strategy substantiates NCM as a business discipline.

Marketers are best placed to provide strategic leadership in the management of this critical interface between the organization and the new marketplace. They oversee the exchange process and the necessary alignment of internal and external factors. They are in the best position to understand and interpret emerging trends for the benefit of the organization.

The New Consumer Marketing model is presented in Figure 5.1, and it shows quite clearly how consumer marketing can be conceptualized as consisting of the three key processes, underpinned by a value-centric orientation. The model is organic in nature, reflected in the use of honeycomb-shaped cells, each of which has a nucleus.

The honeycomb, with its familiar six-sided shape, provides a useful metaphor for explaining how marketing can be visualized as a living demand system. The honey-bee is well known to us all. This is a creature that is renowned for its productivity and the fact that it creates its own value proposition in the form of honey. Honey manufacture is a task shared among various types of bee, and each contributes its own instinctive expertise. The hive members work in harmony to ensure the survival of the colony. Of course, this is just a metaphor and there are limits to how far it can be taken, but because it is dynamic, iterative and flexible, the honeycomb offers an example of working where people and process are combined in a continually productive system.

The capabilities at the heart of each key process and the seven elements that make up the organizational DNA demonstrate the company-wide, high-level approach that is taken by the NCM model. By offering a holistic approach to managing the exchange process in a dynamic marketplace, the model aims to assist managers in developing and implementing successful consumer marketing strategies.

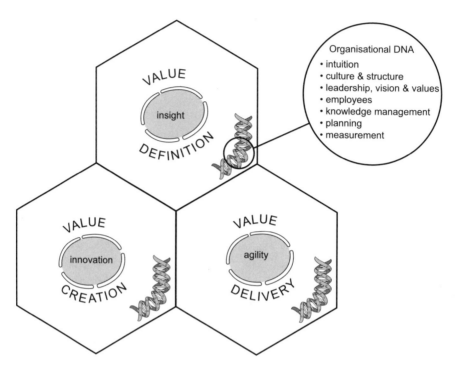

Figure 5.1 The New Consumer Marketing model

The first cell in the demand system is concerned with the process of *value definition*; that is, the process of generating and identifying insight in order to describe and demonstrate value. Chapter 6 covers the traditional and non-traditional ways of generating insight. Segmentation then considers how insight is made actionable. Finally, the importance of re-evaluating the role and status of the insight generators within an organization is explored.

The next cell in the demand system is *value creation*. Chapter 7 explores the process of creating value that results in a value proposition for a specific audience. Innovation forms the nucleus of this cell and the strategic significance of this is covered. Other elements in the process include new product development, branding, positioning and pricing. Branding is portrayed as the consumer's experience of value, and the implications of this are discussed through a number of cases.

The third key process in a demand system is *value delivery*. Chapter 8 discusses how value is communicated and conveyed by an organization to a specific audience. Media and channels are explored, alongside the roles of service, technology integration and supply-chain management. The watchword here is organizational agility.

Finally, Chapter 9 describes the seven elements of the *organizational 'DNA'* that makes a demand system viable. This chapter describes how the cells of the living system are managed through an exploration of the nature and interrelationships of intuition, culture and structure, leadership, vision and values, employees, knowledge management, planning, and measurement. These are the elements that instruct and inform the three cells of the living demand system about how to optimize performance and ensure competitive survival.

Value Definition 6

The process of defining value from the consumer's perspective:

- Defining value = generating and identifying insight in order to describe and demonstrate value specifically
- Watchword = insight

In the production-driven era, marketing was informed by a seller-centric orientation. In today's consumption-led economy, New Consumers are more demanding and sophisticated, and they inhabit an interactive marketplace. Marketing in this business environment requires a different orientation. New Consumer Marketing is founded on a value-centric philosophy that focuses on defining, creating and delivering the value that consumers want to buy into and the organization wants to deliver. The mutuality of the benefits gained by both parties is recognized and a symbiotic relationship is established.

Managing this relationship between organization and New Consumer requires an alternative approach to the command-and-control practices of the production-driven era. Mechanistic models are no longer appropriate and more organic models are being developed, such as the New Consumer Marketing model presented in this book.

Value definition, the first cell in the New Consumer Marketing model, is concerned with the process of defining the value consumers are seeking. Insight forms the cell's nucleus. Insight is described as 'the power of seeing into and understanding things, imaginative penetration, practical knowledge and awareness'. It enables the organization to begin the process of connecting with New Consumers in a way that will deliver sustainable competitive advantage.

In generating knowledge about New Consumers, many organizations claim that the traditional tools and techniques of market research do not seem to be working as well as they did in former times, and marketers are looking to broaden the range they use. The aim is to get underneath the skin of consumers in a way that provides insight into their unarticulated needs and desires. To achieve this, organizations are increasingly adopting a bricolage approach in which investigative and interpretative market research methods drawn from different disciplines are pieced together. In best-practice organizations, the insight generated is applied to the consumer base through the process of segmentation in order to identify the value that is required by the organization's most promising prospects.

THE ROLE OF INSIGHT IN VALUE DEFINITION

Although insight is derived from the obvious, it is not the same as fact. Insight is the capacity to penetrate the human condition and see hidden truths. For example, it is a fact that snowboarding is a sport, but it is an insight that snowboarders are the only sportsmen and women who feel treated like outcasts on the slopes. Where an insight is turned into a compelling marketing idea, it can work to create a powerful bond between the consumer and the brand. Brands of clothing for snowboarders that promote the idea of belonging to a rebellious tribe have been highly successful, for example.

Insight provides the means for defining value from the consumer's perspective. To interpret consumer insight in a way that is meaningful, organizations need to understand what are the component factors that constitute value. These factors will serve one of three purposes for the consumer: they will enhance value, maintain value, or destroy value. This value concept is illustrated in Figure 6.1.

Identifying the Factors that Enhance, Maintain and Destroy Value

Identifying these value-influencing factors and the way in which they interrelate is the fundamental aim of all insight-generation activities. Factors that create or enhance value for the consumer are those that are mould-breaking, or have never before been offered in the marketplace.

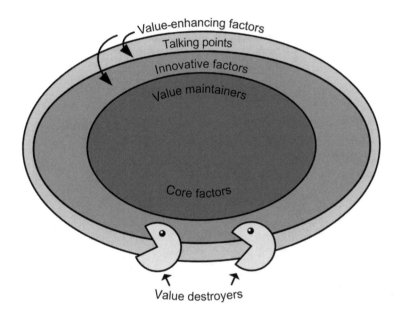

Figure 6.1 The value concept

They are the key discriminating factors that set the organization apart from competitors in the eyes of consumers. Occasionally, these value-enhancers may be 'adopted' by consumers and become 'talking points', creating great word-of-mouth marketing. A good example of this is Krispy Kreme Doughnuts.

Krispy Kreme Doughnuts

Krispy Kreme Doughnuts is one of the top five fastest-growing businesses in the quick-service restaurant sector in North America, with plans for expansion into Europe. Krispy Kreme aficionados swear by the company's hot Original Glazed doughnuts, which are 'manufactured' before the customer's eyes in the Doughnut Theater (a visible conveyor belt-based operation). The Krispy Kreme Doughnut experience receives popular acclaim (including that contributed by cartoon character Homer Simpson, who is famous for his 'Mmm, donuts ...' phrase). This strong word-of-mouth marketing has played a significant role in building consumer awareness of the brand. In Canada, for instance, the impulse to purchase fresh, hot Krispy Kreme doughnuts is so strong that, according to the Canadian marketing director, people will drive, on average, 14 miles to reach a Krispy Kreme store.

Figure 6.2 Krispy Kreme Doughnuts are a talking point
The name Krispy Kreme and the Krispy Kreme Bow-Tie are trademarks of
HDN Development Corp., a subsidiary of Krispy Kreme Doughnut Corporation

Companies offering 'value-enhancers' will build market share quickly, rearranging the competitive forces in the marketplace as they do so. For example, the Woolwich Building Society has seen its business improve at the expense of rivals as a direct consequence of introducing a new kind of account – the Openplan Account. Openplan creates value for customers by placing customers in control of their money and enabling them to manage their complex financial matters easily through using the one account. It allows customers to personalize the names of their various savings 'pots' and to tell the Woolwich when to move funds into higher-interest accounts. For consumers, Openplan was a welcome change from the traditional way of banking where customers would be told how their money was being handled and has now been adopted by the Barclays group of the Woolwich Building Society.

Factors that maintain value are the 'hygiene' factors, or the core features and attributes that all competitors must offer to be considered players in the marketplace. These 'value-maintainers' work in combination with the 'value-enhancers' to affirm value with consumers. They should be subject to regular sense checking to ensure that they continue to perform this supportive role. It may be the case that one or more of these value-maintaining factors has the potential to be developed into a value-enhancing factor. Alternatively, some of these factors may have to be dropped from the offering if they show signs of actually reducing its consumer value.

The third category of factors that make up the consumer's concept of value encompasses those that diminish and destroy value. These are the 'turn-offs' for consumers. Once identified, these 'value-destroyers' should be eliminated from the offering, but not before the company has an understanding of why they have a destructive influence. Their significance can be overlooked where there is not a dynamic approach to generating insight. Laura Ashley's experience provides a useful example.

Laura Ashley

In the early 1990s, Laura Ashley, the fashions and furnishings retail chain, researched the behaviour of its own shoppers and noted that if shoppers made a purchase of curtains, particularly made-to-measure curtains, from the store, they had a higher propensity to go on to buy matching wallpaper and other home furnishing items as well. A £300 purchase could easily become the first of a series of transactions with a combined value of several thousand pounds. The purchase of curtains was, in effect, a trigger to other sales. However, the study revealed that customers were increasingly put off from purchasing curtains when expert staff were not available. This occurred most often on Saturdays when the stores used part-time, relatively inexperienced staff. Clearly, ordering made-to-measure curtains involves some fairly complicated calculations and there is a wide margin for error. Customers would only place an order with someone they believed was competent enough to check their own calculations and order the curtains correctly. Once Laura Ashley realized the impact of its staffing policy, the company made the necessary changes, and this resulted in higher levels of customer satisfaction and greater sales of curtains. By removing this particular value-destroyer, the company was able to uphold its customers' value perceptions of the brand.

Source: H. Peck, 'Relationship Marketing: Lessons from Laura Ashley', case study, Cranfield School of Management, 1995.

In some cases, organizations have a misperception themselves about the factors that create value, spuriously believing that certain factors add value when in fact they simply maintain or even destroy it. These are the 'phantom factors' in the value exchange and can often take on sacred status within a business. For example, the Ford Motor Company believed for a long time that it was necessary to include a spare wheel as part of a new car offering. However, insight generated by its small car product strategy team into the requirements of StreetKa buyers showed that a spare wheel was not important in the purchase decision. With this knowledge, the misgivings of Ford engineers were overcome and the company went on to successfully launch a model without a spare wheel. Drivers are instead supplied with a canister of foam, which will enable them to fix a puncture sufficiently well to drive to the nearest garage for repair or replacement.

Understanding the Meaning of the Value Factors

Having identified the components of value that factor in the consumer's perception of value, the organization then needs to understand exactly what meaning they have for consumers. Consumers typically describe these value factors in terms of tangible or intangible features. The task for marketers is to delve deeper and question why consumers consider these features to be important. The answers will lie in the benefits the features deliver and the way in which some of these benefits, in turn, work at a 'higher level' in satisfying consumers' personal values. Consumer research into how Nike trainers are purchased showed that while the inclusion of the air sole was a straightforward physical feature of the shoe, many consumers considered it to be a value-enhancer. Consumers felt that the cushioning effect of the sole would provide greater comfort and protection on the sports ground and this in turn would enable them to play sport better. The air sole thus satisfied personal values associated with a sense of well-being and keeping fit. In this way, product features, benefits and personal values become interlinked in the consumer's mind. This is shown graphically in Figure 6.3.

Mapping consumer perceptions of products in this way demonstrates why the various components of value are important. It is a technique that can be used to understand how consumers perceive differences between products, revealing to the organization the competitive set in which it operates. Mapping the component factors of value for consumers is based on a well-established research approach known as means–end theory.[1] The theory suggests that consumers make the value exchange as a means of achieving something else. This 'something else' may be about product

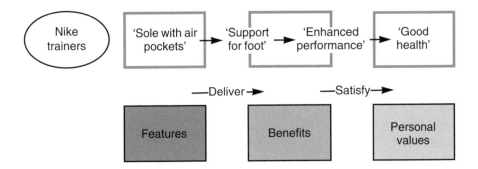

Figure 6.3 Linking features, benefits and personal values

benefits or it may be about the satisfaction of personal values. Uncovering these linkages is key to creating, positioning, communicating and delivering the value offer, as explained in the next chapters.

Insight, then, enables the organization to define value from the consumer's perspective. It provides a means of identifying underlying sources of buyer motivation. Current thinking as to how this process of generating insight should be undertaken is in a state of flux as traditional market research is being augmented with a range of alternative practices.

THE ROLE OF TRADITIONAL MARKET RESEARCH IN VALUE DEFINITION

In seeking to get closer to New Consumers, marketing managers today have an expanding box of tools and techniques at their disposal. These generally fall into one of two categories: traditional market research, and non-traditional approaches to market sensing. The former comprises established practices, which are being updated by new thinking from various disciplines. The latter includes a range of approaches from old-fashioned reliance on front-line staff to the contemporary use of IT.

As the staple method of insight generation, market research aims to answer fundamental questions about what makes consumers 'tick' so that managers can refine existing marketing practice. Market research emerged as a formalized business process in the latter part of the last century, although the principles it encapsulates go back much further. The prime objective of the modern survey, a standard tool of market research, is to recapture the 'dialogue' that took place between buyer and seller in the pre-industrial age where the local market or village shop dominated as the place of buyer–seller interactions.

Formalized market research was first undertaken by manufacturers in the fast moving consumer goods (fmcg) sector. It enabled companies to gain a structured and reliable view of the marketplace, which they could then use to improve their competitiveness. They studied markets by borrowing the statistical methods and principles developed by social scientists to understand and quantify human behaviour. They used these in combination with the sampling methods they already had in place to ensure quality control on their production lines. Some of the earliest books on the subject of market research were, in fact, published by leading brand owners such as Cadbury and Shell. These books were used as internal training manuals in the days before comprehensive reference texts were available. The tools and techniques developed then still form the staple of most market research plans today. What is changing is the mix of techniques used: qualitative approaches are slowly gaining ground at the expense of quantitative approaches.

Using Quantitative Research

Generating insight means focusing largely on answering the 'why' question: 'why do people do/think/buy what they do/think/buy?'. Data on 'who, what, where, when and how many', on the other hand, provides useful information on context. To generate this data, organizations usually fall back on the use of quantitative surveys. These routinely involve large numbers of respondents, who may be chosen on a quota basis to create a statistically representative selection of the larger population. Respondents are all asked the same questions in highly structured interviews to establish evidence of market preferences and trends. Quantitative surveys can be conducted on an ad hoc or ongoing basis – the latter are often referred to as panel surveys. Ad hoc surveys can provide insight into a potential solution to a specific business issue, and may be repeated on 'fresh' groups of respondents at regular intervals. For example, Wall's Ice Cream publishes an annual survey on the topic of children's pocket money. Panel surveys, on the other hand, use the same set of respondents to provide regular (weekly or monthly) feedback on grocery purchases, for example. Data is collected in four main ways: by post, by telephone, in face-to-face interviews and, increasingly, via web-based surveys.

While many marketing managers profess a preference for quantitative surveys simply because they contain 'hard numbers' based on the science of statistics and sampling theory, the pivotal issue is the robustness of the data evidence. David Smith and Jonathon Fletcher (2001) suggest there are seven questions to be answered before reassurance can be given:

- Was the design free of flaws?
- Was the sample representative?
- Did the questionnaire 'work'?
- Was the process free of interviewer bias?
- Were there any data preparation errors?
- Were there any presentation and/or reporting errors?
- Was the interpretation free of flaws?

This traditional quantitative approach to research essentially deals with averages; it tells marketers what an average consumer wants. But finding average consumers is difficult. As is often quoted, some consumers like iced tea, others like hot tea, but very few express a liking for lukewarm tea. This practice of looking for 'averages' is typical of an aggregate way of thinking and, as has been made clear so far in this book, markets today are disaggregated and characterized by high levels of heterogeneity. The New Consumer cannot be described as 'average'. To generate meaningful insight into consumer needs and preferences, researchers are turning to a greater use of qualitative approaches.

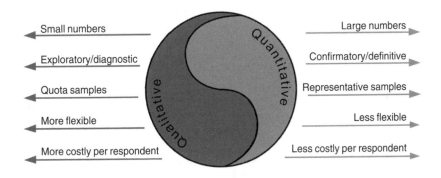

Figure 6.4 Qualitative versus quantitative research

Using Qualitative Research

In seeking to answer the 'why' question, researchers increasingly draw on an eclectic pot-pourri of qualitative techniques. The roots of qualitative research can be traced to the 1960s, the height of the production-driven era, when marketers began to demand deeper insights into the purchasing behaviour of consumers and motivational research, an approach developed by Ernest Dichter, gave birth to contemporary qualitative methods of enquiry. In effect, the consumer was 'put on the couch' and the researcher's interpretations of attitudes and behaviour were drawn from the fields of psychology and psychoanalysis. Projective questioning ('if this brand were an animal, what kind of animal would it be?') and other techniques adapted from these disciplines became the favoured tools for mainstream qualitative researchers. Over the next two decades researchers from other disciplines, such as sociology and social anthropology, added their contributions, introducing notions of humankind as social animals and as products of their culture.

Today, traditional qualitative research commonly features the use of focus groups and in-depth interviews. These methods involve asking comparatively small samples of respondents questions about what they do and think, and listening to and interpreting the response. The output of qualitative research is exploratory or diagnostic in nature; respondents are not meant to be representative of the larger population, but are intended to reflect the profile of known or desired consumers. (Non-consumers are also often consulted for their independent input.) The aim is to generate understanding of the things that bind groups of consumers together.

Sadly, the impressionistic and non-confirmatory nature of qualitative research has received bad press over recent years, to an extent where focus groups have become demonized in some quarters of the national media. Small-sample statistical theory has never been robust enough to convince many managers that the evidence produced by 36 or 48 people is as accurate as the aggregated output of 2,000 survey respondents. There is often confusion over the way in which the evidence should be used to shape the strategy of an organization. However, the notion that it is acceptable to work with limited numbers of respondents is an accepted method in the social sciences. Grounded Theory,[2] as this concept is known, states that researchers should stop collecting fresh information when they get to a point where it ceases to add anything to the conceptual understanding of the issue under investigation (usually after conducting a limited number of interviews).

These traditional approaches to quantitative and qualitative research are based on an assumption that consumers can – and are willing to – articulate their thoughts, beliefs, feelings and behaviours. Organizations wanting to make breakthrough developments are rather more concerned with understanding latent, unarticulated consumer wants and desires. To meet this demand on the part of organizations, researchers have added to the toolbox more 'in situ' investigative methods, such as discourse, semiotic and ethnographic analyses. These provide a deeper understanding of the meaning of value factors to consumers, bringing organizations closer to the 'Aha!' moment when insight becomes obvious.

Discourse Analysis

Discourse analysis is a market research technique that looks for patterns in people's language, such as the metaphors or figures of speech they use to communicate about the world around them. It can also mean undertaking a review of individual words to gain a deep understanding of what consumers mean when they say something. Discourse analysis demands a detailed examination of every utterance, including those that are traditionally discarded in the process of analysis. This would include how respondents use what linguists refer to as 'discourse markers' (non-semantic, syntactically empty words, such as 'like', 'um', 'er', 'kind of', 'sort of', 'you know' in the English language) as they are often carriers of cultural meaning. Insight into how consumers use language can help marketers connect more effectively with consumers as they can use consumers' own language in creating and delivering value. One of the most outstanding examples of a business that was built on an insightful understanding of consumers' language is the most successful pre-school television programme ever produced – Teletubbies.

Teletubbies

Teletubbies was developed by Anne Wood and Andrew Davenport for Ragdoll Ltd. Anne Wood's inspirational talent has earned her a multi-million pound empire and an international reputation for pioneering work in children's television. The success of the original idea can be traced to a combination of Wood's ideas and business acumen, and Davenport's expertise in language development and his acute observations of the world of young children. The brightly coloured characters soon established themselves as firm favourites among pre-school children and their parents, with their empathetic use of the pre-schooler's language and their universal comic appeal.

Figure 6.5 The *Teletubbies* online

Teletubbies characters and logo © & ™ 1996 Ragdoll Ltd. Licensed by BBC Worldwide Ltd

Semiotics Analysis

Another set of techniques for generating insight draws on the discipline of semiotics. This is the science of decoding cultural signs, which is used by researchers to get into consumers' subconscious and to predict where consumer trends are heading. It is based on a belief that we are all shaped by our culture (and not the other way round), and that goods are charged with cultural meaning. Consumers use this meaning as a form of expression to say something about themselves, to develop and sustain their lifestyles, and to create and sustain social change. The role of the researcher is to decode the symbols as a way of understanding culture and what consumers are saying about themselves. This kind of insight provides managers with a means of understanding the role of brands within a culture, both the organization's own brands and competitive offerings. The well-established drinks brand Guinness has successfully employed semiotics analysis.

Guinness

Guinness UDV tasked Malcolm Evans and the Added Value agency with developing a user-friendly marketing tool that could be used around the world to gain insight into the competitive environment (Evans, 2001). Using semiotics analysis, Evans and his team created a tool kit that guides marketers in various local markets through the same process. This enables them to map an understanding of the meaning of beer to consumers in each of their markets, and then to analyse and interpret the advertisements in order to understand the advertising proposition. Having decoded the market, Guinness executives can then work on refining the positioning of their brands in that market.

Ethnographic Analysis

A third approach to generating insight into consumers' latent wants and desires that is arousing a lot of interest is brand ethnography. This is based on a technique developed in the social sciences in the late nineteenth and early twentieth centuries where researchers went overseas to research traditional 'tribes' and cultures. The underlying philosophy of ethnographic analysis is that the closer the researcher can get to consumers' habitats, the greater the chance he or she has of understanding consumers' relationships with other people or with the things that surround them. It is based on a central belief that the researcher's study of consumer behaviour is most accurate and revealing when consumers are immersed in their natural environment.

This approach to generating insight means taking an analytical view of consumers over a long period of time. Longitudinal studies, as they are known, are not common in marketing because of the high costs involved and because research results are generally required sooner than an ethnographic study can deliver them. However, some companies, such as Unilever, consider the investment worthwhile.

Unilever

Unilever used this ethnographic analysis to understand the opportunities arising from the growth of sales of white goods in developing countries. The results of its year-long study identified broad areas of opportunity, for example, the types of clothes bought and worn, how clothes are treated and cared for, and consumer expectations of clothes care and product benefits. All of this was set within a cultural context. The study also identified a structured framework of issues that the company had not previously been aware of, to do with attitudes and behaviours relating to the process of caring for clothes. This new knowledge presented an opportunity to focus subsequent research more closely on these issues, with the aim of uncovering some latent wants and desires that were not being satisfied. This later research opened up new commercial opportunities for Unilever.

Source: Lynn McKay, New Futures Consumer Scientist, 'Creating commercial value from ethnographic insights', presented at the Generating and Leveraging Consumer Insight Conference, IQPC, London, March 2002.

As with more standard approaches to qualitative research, these three analytical methods – discourse, semiotic and ethnographic analysis – are not designed to be representative of the wider population of consumers, but are intended instead to generate insight that could never be uncovered through focus groups, in-depth interviews and quantitative surveys. Critics suggest the techniques are very dependent on the interpretational skills of the individual researcher, can often appear to be using a sledgehammer to crack a nut, and tend to produce more data than is usefully required. However, these research techniques can reveal frameworks for further consumer analysis, leading to meaningful understanding of the value consumers are seeking, within a wider cultural context.

Need-States Analysis

As the consumption-led economy becomes more of a reality for organizations, debate about how best to generate insight into consumer–brand relationships moves on apace. In 1994, qualitative research expert Wendy Gordon revived the concept of need-states to explain the fact that there are more differences between the same consumer making a brand choice on two different occasions, than between two different consumers choosing the same brand on the same occasion. People choose brands to fit a particular context. For example, consumers may choose to buy a cheaper bottle of supermarket own-label wine from the supermarket to drink with a partner at home, yet they will choose a more expensive shipper's labelled wine to take as a gift when dining at a friend's house. Their choice of product is influenced by a variety of factors, including the meaning of each occasion, the environment in which the wine will be consumed, and the other people involved. This leads to the idea that a brand can be positioned against a need-state, and through effective brand communications activity can become the brand most associated with that need-state.

Need-states analysis has at its core an understanding of how consumers make sense of the world. Consumers create a model of the world in their minds, which psychologists refer to as a 'mental model'. It is the consumer's representation of how something is or how something happens. A brand can be thought of as a type of mental model, and this subject is discussed further in the next chapter. However, the notion of mental models is relevant here as the task of the researcher is one of uncovering consumers' mental models of the world. Thinking about consumer–brand relationships in this way draws on learning from cognitive science, the branch of psychology that deals with how the mind works from the individual's perspective.

Today, Wendy Gordon firmly believes that the future of cognitive science lies in the newly merged disciplines of neuroscience and cognitive psychology, known as neuro-psychology (Gordon, 2001). This branch of learning brings together an understanding of the science of the brain, its physiology and functions, as well as psychological theories. For her, this emerging discipline offers the opportunity to truly get inside the consumer's mind. She believes it holds the promise of a scientific basis for understanding how human beings create, store, recall and relate to brands in everyday life.

What is evident from this discussion of the role of traditional (quantitative and qualitative) market research in generating insight is that organizations cannot rely on only one of the techniques to deliver absolute insight. The reality is that both quantitative and qualitative research offer meaningful insight and they work in complementary ways. As Gordon says in her book on qualitative research, *Goodthinking* (1999), 'The case for using bricolage (a pieced together set of investigative and interpretative methods drawn from different disciplines) has never been stronger'. Approaches to bricolage also draw on non-traditional market sensing techniques, and these are considered next.

THE ROLE OF NON-TRADITIONAL MARKET SENSING IN VALUE DEFINITION

While market research provides a stream of invaluable knowledge about consumers, it is increasingly augmented with information derived from the use of database systems and technology that enables front-line staff to provide instant feedback on consumer behaviour. This data works in a supplementary fashion, providing the organization with the opportunity to develop a more complete understanding of consumer motivation. This understanding is vital for constructing successful value propositions.

Using Database Systems

In the 1970s traditional market research methods were the only real source of consumer insight. By the 1990s, marketers were becoming spoilt for choice as data flowed in ever greater quantities from scanners, loyalty schemes, satisfaction surveys, service requests, account information and so on. The challenge facing organizations today is how to fuse data in meaningful ways so that a holistic, or 360-degree, picture of consumers is created. This means understanding how and in what ways an individual consumer interacts with an organization over time. It entails building a corporate memory of the consumer so that the call centre agent is aware that the customer on the telephone wrote to the company's head office two months earlier and that a subsequent home visit from a member of the customer services team went well. Achieving a corporate memory means adopting the philosophy that every encounter with consumers is a mutual learning experience. If they do this, organizations can better manage relationships and, in turn, customer profitability.

Customer databases built up through loyalty card schemes enable organizations to turn consumer information into knowledge and to transform that knowledge into actionable propositions that provide consumer benefits. These benefits strengthen the consumer's bond with the company. From the company's point of view, a loyalty scheme that simply rewards the consumer but ignores the vital flow of information provided by each transaction is a sales promotion scheme however large it might be. Loyalty card information, when mined effectively, can reveal to the company the distinct and different groups of consumers it serves. In Tesco's case, loyalty card data is central to the way in which the business is run.

Tesco Clubcard

Tesco Clubcard was introduced in February 1995 and today has over 10 million active members. Although its start-up costs were high (judged by analysts to be in the region of £10 million in addition to the 1% discount on sales, estimated at £60 million), take-up of the loyalty card was significant. Within one month of its launch over 5 million people had joined the scheme and Tesco recorded a 7% increase in like-for-like sales. This propelled Tesco to overtake Sainsbury's as Britain's leading retailer of packaged goods.

Over the years, Tesco has learned how to manage Clubcard data for maximum strategic effect. The company admits to having been overwhelmed initially at the deluge of data generated by the scheme. Clubcard had effectively opened up a dialogue with members, and hundreds of letters and up to 30,000 phone calls a week had to be dealt with. Specialist data management consultants were brought in to manage the communication process until Tesco's own in-house team had built up the necessary expertise. In fact, data-mining skills are so strongly valued at Tesco that the data analysis firm engaged to analyse Clubcard data is now a subsidiary of Tesco.

David Reid, Tesco's deputy chairman, has claimed that 'It's very easy to malign loyalty cards. People are always rubbishing them because of the expense. But if you took our loyalty cards away from us, it would be like flying blind. They tell us how to attract customers, how secondary customers behave, how specific customers react to specific promotions, how you can influence competitors' openings, how you can spot new trends, how you can convert customers' (Child, 2002).

Source: 'Tesco Clubcard Forever?', case study, H. Peck, Cranfield School of Management, 2002.

Using CRM Systems

The introduction of Tesco Clubcard demonstrates that effective customer relationship management (CRM) systems are not just about automating or speeding up operations. They are also about using data and information to intelligently manage customer relationships. Tesco and other organizations have learned how to benefit from collecting and mining data, as well as using other techniques such as analytic profiling, segmentation and predictive analyses to identify individuals and uncover consumer preferences and propensities (so that optimal profitability can be attained). However, despite the extent of the analysis provided by a CRM system, it is only market research that can provide a qualitative perspective. Major CRM system vendors, such as Siebel Systems, Oracle, SAP and Peoplesoft, are working on introducing analytical tools to enable their client companies to understand their customers better in this way.

The problem in practice is that mechanisms for generating both quantitative and qualitative customer understanding have not been a part of the historical development of CRM systems. This is because the development of databases to hold behavioural customer data has usually been managed in organizations as a parallel process to that of market research. This way of operating evolved during the production-driven era. In the new marketplace of the consumption-led economy, insight generation is looked upon as a total process, one that encompasses both traditional and non-traditional market sensing processes. What is important is using consumer insight to inform strategic decisions that impact value creation and delivery.

It should also be noted that fusing data from multiple sources raises ethical as well as technological issues. These issues arise because data that has been gathered anonymously for use in attitudinal and lifestyle surveys can now be fused together with loyalty card data that has been collected together with full personal details. In the process of fusion it becomes possible to identify those individuals who gave their data anonymously. This makes them vulnerable to marketing approaches by companies and raises an ethical dilemma for the market researcher, who would have given an assurance to an individual respondent that the data would be handled confidentially, implying any personal details would not be used by the organization. Overall, the market research industry has been careful in treading on what they perceive to be a potential landmine of personal privacy. This is acting as a brake on industry efforts to leverage multiple forms of data to generate total consumer insight.

To deal with ethical issues, professional codes of conduct relating to the practice of market research were first established in the early 1960s: in Europe, by ESOMAR (a European association of market research professionals), in association with the International Chambers of Commerce, and in the UK, by the Market Research Society. The key principle in both sets of standards and in other codes of research practice worldwide is consumer confidentiality. The identities of survey participants are not disclosed in analysis or reporting processes. The protection of consumer confidentiality encourages respondents to provide honest responses about their attitudes and opinions. It also serves to protect them from unsolicited marketing approaches.

In Europe today, the professional bodies are working together with EU legislators to find a way of regulating data protection. The US and other key nations, however, have yet to enact any laws on data privacy, thereby creating a potential minefield for global players.

Using Front-line Staff

Finally, insight can also be generated using a combination of front-line staff and cutting-edge information technology. Zara, the Spanish fashion company that is rapidly expanding globally, provides a useful example of the way in which insight generated on the shop floor can be used to create and deliver value for consumers in a seamless process. Zara's strategy is built on having a value-centric orientation in the business, where insight provides a continual flow of opportunity. (Zara is also referred to later in Chapter 8, and the management of employees, including front-line staff, is covered in Chapter 9.)

Zara

In a sector where the average high-street retailer predicts trends often a year or more in advance, Zara can turn a trend around in a matter of days. This is partly because it has its own factories and also because of the emphasis it places on communication between the shop floor and the factory floor. As Zara UK's managing director, Michael Shearwood, points out, 'We don't try to persuade customers to buy something we make. We sell products that the customer wants to buy'. Store managers are offered fashion collections twice a week and they can select items according to what they feel will suit their particular customers. They can also communicate specific customer fashion desires to Zara's Spanish headquarters up to four times a day using handheld keypads. A few days later, the requested clothes are delivered to the store concerned.

The deployment of IT at the front line, where it can directly impact customer satisfaction, was ably demonstrated in one case involving a white blouse. The shirt was delivered to UK stores bearing decorative epaulettes. The shirts did not sell. Feedback from customers indicated that women preferred the shirt plain, without the epaulettes. This information was passed on to the shirt factory, which promptly manufactured an amended version and sent it out to the UK stores, whereupon it became a best seller.

In order to know what trends are about to emerge, Zara employs a team of about 200 designers, dubbed the 'creation team'. They travel around the world and their task is to gather vital fashion intelligence from clubs, discos, university campuses and catwalks. The affordable clothes sold by the Zara manufacturing and retail chain have become popular among leading fashion editors, who revere their quality, fashionability and value-for-money prices.

Source: Based on 'The mark of Zara', Linda Watson, *Style Magazine*, 2001.

THE ROLE OF SEGMENTATION IN VALUE DEFINITION

In best practice organizations, consumer insight is turned into marketing action through the process of consumer segmentation. By segmenting consumers into groups sharing the same or similar needs on the basis of value, as defined in their own terms, an organization can acquire up-to-the-minute understanding of its consumer base. This can then be used to develop more cost-effective consumer strategies. Because consumer perceptions of value change, it is important that both value definition and consumer segmentation are undertaken on a regular and frequent basis. Organizations that can quickly react to change and anticipate shifts in the value demands of consumers have a head start on their competitors. Such flexibility and focus on demand lie at the heart of New Consumer Marketing.

Much of the current discussion about segmentation is informed by the mechanistic approach of the production-driven era. This is characterized by the use of scientific and rational language and focuses on the way in which the organization should segment *its* market, i.e. 'chop it up' into manageable chunks. The reality of the consumption-led economy is that consumers themselves unwittingly form loose groups whose members are seeking the same or similar sets of value factors. In other words, consumers segment *their* market and form subgroups with *their* own sets of requirements. The language associated with segmentation today is more to do with creativity and insight, as organizations wrestle with the challenge of finding a means of exposing these segments of consumers and defining the value that each is seeking.

The process of value definition enables the organization to be confident about the market in which it operates. Segmentation provides the answer to the simple but strategic question, 'What business are we in?'. The importance of answering this question correctly was highlighted back in 1960 by Theodore Levitt in his seminal work, *Marketing Myopia*, in which he draws attention to the importance of viewing a business in a way that is appropriate to the markets in which it operates. His classic example involved the railroads, which defined themselves as being in the railway business, rather than in the transportation business. 'The railroads did not stop growing because the need for passenger and freight transportation declined. That grew. The railroads are in trouble today not because the need was filled by others (cars, trucks, aeroplanes, even telephones), but because it was not filled by the railroads themselves.' The railroad companies had a product-driven view of the marketplace and failed to see that the value their customers were looking for was more to do with the benefits derived from transportation and communication than what the railroads simply had to offer.

Today, too many businesses still define and segment their markets in terms of the products they sell. Personal financial services companies, for example, typically take this product-driven approach, defining markets as 'endowment policies', 'savings bonds' or 'savings accounts'. They fail to understand the kinds of value their customers are seeking, such as the desire to save for retirement, support a child through higher education, or simply have peace of mind.

Correct market definition is crucial to the development of a value-centric orientation as it links directly with the mission, vision and values of the company. It enables the organization to accurately articulate what it aims to achieve, and to measure its market share and market growth against relevant competitors as it does so. These issues are considered further in Chapter 9.

Creating a Segmentation Analysis

Customer databases built up through loyalty card schemes, such as those operated by the major supermarkets, can provide a rich source of information on buying behaviour. However, it should always be remembered that a segmentation analysis built solely on this sort of data

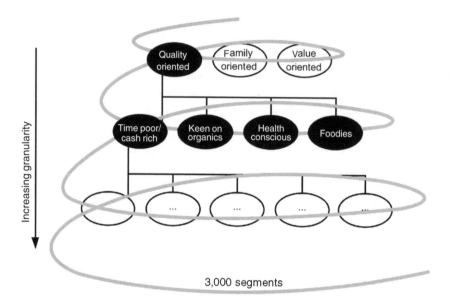

Figure 6.6 Segmenting consumer markets: a hypothetical supermarket example

can only reflect the motivations of existing customers. It becomes a *database* segmentation and not any form of *market* segmentation. Meaningful segmentation analysis takes into consideration different types of data.

In terms of the ideal number of clusters or segments to aim for in a segmentation analysis, the recommendation used to be no more than half a dozen, but developments in data analysis and data fusion mean that companies can now work with a greater number. Figure 6.6 illustrates how this larger number can arise.

A major supermarket may start with a small number of 'super segments' and then subdivide these further until it has reached a large but manageable number of micro-segments. Developments in IT make the management of large numbers of segments possible. For example, three super segments may be uncovered in the segmentation analysis: shoppers who are quality oriented, family oriented and value oriented. These super segments could then be further subdivided into a larger number of sub-segments known as 'category one segments'. The quality-oriented segment, for example, might be made up of four sub-segments: time-poor/cash-rich shoppers, health conscious shoppers, shoppers with a preference for organic foods, and 'foodies', or shoppers who favour fine foods. In this way the segmentation process would be continued, building on insight generated through both traditional and non-traditional research approaches, until an optimum number of segments is reached. The optimum number of segments is reached when each segment is of an adequate size to provide the company with the desired return on investment, members of the segment share a high degree of similarity in their requirements yet are distinct from the rest of the market, the segments are reachable, and they can be serviced by the organization in terms of value creation and value delivery.

Today, in the UK, the major supermarkets would typically work at a high level of segment granularity, with up to as many as 3,000 segments cascaded down from their overarching super segments. One-to-one marketing may be talked about as a viable aim but the commercial reality is rather different, as for most organizations the costs of delivering this outweigh the returns. The challenge is to find new analytic approaches to subdividing the market to an acceptable level of granularity. These more contemporary approaches to segmentation keep managerial focus on understanding the value sought by the individual segments, and do so in a way that prevents consumer profiling from becoming a barrier to consumer understanding. Where an organization talks in terms of only four or five consumer profiles, these can actually hinder an organization's ability to deal with the high levels of heterogeneity characteristic of the new marketplace.

Having identified its different consumer segments, the organization can then move on to evaluate which segments offer the best business opportunities. Segments may be assessed in terms of market size and market trends, market share, current and future profitability, consumer satisfaction, and/or consumer loyalty. Companies usually manage a portfolio of segments, made up of high earners, steady earners and future potential earners. Any low earners need to be managed carefully – often, a small increase in the number of times consumers forming this segment make a purchase can result in large improvements to the bottom line.

Finally, continuing with this supermarket segmentation example, the analysis could then be used to understand the shopper profile of existing stores and to define value, for example, through ascertaining what percentage of consumers in each of the category one segments frequents particular store types (e.g. large format versus convenience) or by location (out-of-town versus high-street stores). The resultant insight could be used to specify new store developments and hence tailor the value offering more closely to the wants and needs of consumers. Given that CRM systems can provide constant streams of up-to-date consumer data, segmentation analyses can become a dynamic part of a demand system. A recent project jointly undertaken by Sainsbury's and Procter & Gamble demonstrates this point.

Sainsbury's and Procter & Gamble

In an innovative example of collaborative effort, Sainsbury's and Procter & Gamble worked together to exploit the wealth of data contained within Sainsbury's Reward Card database in order to deliver a holistic segmentation analysis of the health and beauty care (H&BC) shopper. Their study linked actual purchasing behaviour to attitudinal data using a big base sample. In the UK, the H&BC market was worth almost £11 billion in 2002 and is forecast to grow 21% to 2006, with Sainsbury's occupying third place behind Boots and Tesco for sales. A major challenge facing Sainsbury's is the difference between the H&BC shopper and the grocery shopper. Shoppers at Sainsbury's are typically aged 45 years plus, while the H&BC shopper is generally younger. Also, the overall store shopper is more upmarket than the Sainsbury's H&BC shopper.

Using loyalty card data, Sainsbury's identified eight segments of shoppers based on their purchasing affinity to different product categories within the H&BC aisle. To complement this understanding, two additional pieces of research were jointly carried out to provide data on the wider H&BC shopping context. Both Sainsbury's shoppers and non-shoppers of the H&BC category were surveyed quantitatively in order to gain insights that would enable Sainsbury's to build greater penetration among non-shoppers and strengthen shopper loyalty among existing shoppers.

Analysis of this data produced a rich source of insight that enabled both parties to learn what each of the segments was looking for in terms of H&BC products, their loyalty to Sainsbury's, who they perceived as the competition, and the type of marketing activity they preferred. The segmentation analysis resulted in actionable results for both Sainsbury's and Procter & Gamble, which were then exploited jointly and separately. The H&BC strategy that was subsequently developed encompassed both existing and new shoppers' needs, and helped grow Sainsbury's H&BC category ahead of the market.

Source: Roger Allford, Natalie Evans and Caroline Ward, 'A step forward in understanding shoppers using segmentation techniques', paper presented at the ESOMAR Conference, 'Consolidation or renewal?', Barcelona, September 2002.

As this case example shows, an organization's approach to segmentation is about more than the analytical techniques it employs. It makes a statement about the organization's market orientation, the way it sees the marketplace and how well it understands the consumers it chooses to serve. Segmentation enables the organization to create competitive advantage for itself by defining value in a way that makes clear how it can profitably create greater value for consumers. New Consumers raise many challenges for organizations and, as this chapter demonstrates, they are impacting the way in which insight into their needs and desires is generated. This, in turn, raises questions about the role and status of the insight generators within a business.

THE ROLE OF INSIGHT GENERATORS[3] IN VALUE DEFINITION

An acceptance of the vital importance of insight to successful New Consumer Marketing makes it necessary to review the role and status of those people within the organization who are generating the insight. These are traditionally staff who are members of the market research team. However, given the wider understanding of how insight can best be generated, this classification should also include those responsible for the analysis of CRM data. All too often, market research is perceived to be a low-grade, commodity business with an output that does not go beyond completing surveys. As commentators said over ten years ago, there is a need to prove that market research is about more than clipboards and opinion polls.

If insight generators are to assume a real decision-making role, then they need to be equipped with a skill set that enables them to draw on the most effective combination of data generation services externally as well as an ability to communicate the learning internally. These insight managers must become proactive consultants within their organizations rather than acting as simple, reactive service providers. They need to ensure that the insight generated becomes the dynamic cornerstone of all marketing activities. In best-practice organizations, this appears to be happening. However, there are, perhaps, too many junior managers joining the market research profession who are not being trained to take on this enhanced role. This can only lead to the marginalization of the profession over time.

Insight generators therefore occupy what is known as a 'boundary-spanning' role in the New Consumer Marketing model. These are staff who 'connect an informal network with other parts of the company or with similar networks in other organizations' (Cross and Prusak, 2002). They operate at the periphery of the organization and their roles are strategically important as facilitators of linkage between the cells of a demand system. It is through their behaviour that the organization adapts (or fails to adapt) to changes in the marketplace. In short, they function as 'sensory organs'. As this role is seldom recognized within organizations, there is no one title that identifies these influential staff.

These boundary-spanning managers are charged with generating a dynamic flow of insight so that insight generation becomes an ongoing process and is not simply seen as an annual or six monthly exercise. They are responsible for ensuring that this insight informs the other two cells of the New Consumer Marketing model through the organization's approach to knowledge management (as explored in Chapter 9). Gaining a momentum in insight generation enables the organization to create a living demand system as it gains a continuous source of insight on which to focus its value creation and delivery processes. The benefits of this process approach to insight generation are that brands can retain their currency with consumers as the organization adapts to shifts in consumer perceptions of value. This ability of an organization to shift in line with changing consumer perceptions of value is well demonstrated in the cases of Lucozade and Skoda.

Lucozade and Skoda

Lucozade's success in the drinks industry is underpinned by its expertise in reading value trends and responding to them appropriately. The Lucozade brand has shifted from being a soft drink aimed at people who are unwell, summed up in the strapline 'Lucozade aids recovery', to a sports drink that 'replaces lost energy', to today's competition-conscious brand that serves as an 'energy boost'.

Car manufacturer Skoda has worked in a similar fashion to remain relevant to consumers. VW, its parent company, acquired the brand in 1991 and has invested in it alongside its other marques, Volkswagen, Audi and Seat. The value associated with Skoda vehicles has changed dramatically; from one that was the butt of jokes to one that gains consumer trust. Skoda's popularity today builds on a simple but clever message: 'We've changed, can you?'.

This first cell of the New Consumer Marketing model is concerned with the process of defining the value consumers are seeking. Value definition drives the demand system by generating relevant insight that provides a focus for the processes of value creation and value delivery. To achieve value definition, organizations are increasingly adopting a bricolage approach that pieces together investigative and interpretative methods drawn from different disciplines.

SUMMARY POINTS

- Insight provides the means of defining value from the consumer's perspective.

- Consumer perceptions of value shift over time. Adopting an ongoing, dynamic approach to insight generation ensures that the organization's perspective of the marketplace does not remain fixed in time.

- Value is made up of component factors that work to enhance, maintain and destroy value. Certain value-enhancers may be adopted by consumers as talking points, delivering valuable word-of-mouth marketing.

- Insight generation is a total process, encompassing traditional market research and non-traditional market sensing.

- Insight is made actionable through the process of segmentation, which helps the organization answer the question 'what business are we in?'.

- Segmentation enables an organization to achieve competitive advantage by clarifying how it can create greater value for consumers.

- Insight generators have an influential boundary-spanning role within the organization and should be valued as 'sensory organs'.

Value Creation 7

The process of creating value resulting in a value proposition for a specific audience:

- Creating value = bringing into being or form, or investing with new form
- Watchword = innovation

Value creation in the consumption-led economy must be informed by an understanding of the value that consumers are looking for and assessed in terms of consumers' value criteria. Satisfying consumer demand today is about winning the custom of discerning consumers and not simply producing good products. This second cell of the New Consumer Marketing model is a fundamental component of a demand system as it moves the organization from defining value to actually creating and communicating that value effectively.

Key to the process of creating value in the marketplace is identifying and utilizing the organization's value-producing resources (e.g. employees, technological know-how and capital) to meet consumer needs and expectations profitably. At the heart of this process is the concept of innovation. Derived from the Latin word *innovare*, meaning to renew or alter, innovation in consumer marketing is about creating new solutions that offer real value to consumers. In many organizations, innovation has become separated from marketing, giving rise, in part, to the crisis in marketing. New Consumer Marketing, with its emphasis on market-led innovation, recombines the two and provides a means of addressing both the demands of New Consumers and the concerns of brand owners and retailers.

The desired output of the value creation process is a value proposition that consumers want to buy into and the organization wants to deliver. The value proposition sets out the value exchange between buyer and supplier, and reinforces the mutuality of the relationship. As stated in Chapter 6, the construction of a successful value proposition depends on first being able to define value by generating relevant insight into consumer demand and the relative attractiveness of different consumer segments. The organization can then work to create this value, and, ultimately, to deliver it.

In building a value proposition out of the value-producing resources of the organization, there are a number of elements to consider. These include new product development, branding, positioning and price. Each plays an important role in the value creation process. Of paramount importance, however, is the role of innovation, for innovation is what underpins the success of all the elements of value creation.

THE ROLE OF INNOVATION IN VALUE CREATION

> The business has two and only these two basic functions: marketing and innovation. Marketing and innovation produce results, all the rest are costs.
>
> (Peter Drucker, 1985)

In the opening chapter of this book, marketing was presented as a discipline in crisis, whose contribution to business is in question. This stems from the fact that many managers see marketing as a cost rather than an investment, and this itself is driven by the lack of a common approach to measuring marketing effectiveness (a subject considered further in Chapter 9). The issue for many managers today is that marketing no longer appears to be delivering innovation; somehow, the two have become separated. New Consumer Marketing, which places innovation at the core of value creation, offers a way of putting strategic intent back into marketing, and so providing a means of lifting marketing out of its crisis.

The value-centric organization is marked by a corporate environment that seeks performance improvement through superior value definition, creation and delivery. Innovation in business provides a way of creating new value-producing resources or endowing existing ones with an enhanced potential for yielding profit. It is the result of a complex set of processes, involving organizational learning, culture, leadership and management style. Innovation is important on a macro-economic level because it is associated with high rates of economic growth and high levels of employment. Within individual firms, innovation enhances organizational performance. The commercial significance of innovation is supported by the findings of PricewaterhouseCoopers (1999), which surveyed 80 companies in seven countries in 1999. It found that new products and services introduced in the preceding five years accounted for a 10% increase in turnover and generated a 2.5% increase in the annual rate of revenue growth. It also found that new products and services were associated with a 9% increase in annual total shareholder returns.

While the firm that innovates first in a market obtains the early mover advantage, this is only sustainable while competitors cannot imitate or neutralize its lead. To stay ahead, the firm must ensure that innovation is a dynamic capability fully embedded within the culture of the organization. The roots of culture lie hidden in the deep-seated collection of beliefs and assumptions that are commonly held in an organization. They are reflected in everyday life as 'the way things get done around here'. Innovation should not be treated simply as a series of individual projects, but as a continuous search for opportunities to improve the value proposition to such an extent that new market space is opened up. A value-centric orientation provides the foundation for achieving this.

Because of the clear business benefits of having an innovative approach to value creation, innovation is something of a holy grail for businesses. This is especially true for brand owners and retailers, who find themselves having to rethink their strategies in line with the macro-market shift from a production-driven to a consumption-led economy. As discussed in Chapter 3, brand owners are looking for improvements in brand performance that will give them an opportunity to assert their position with retailers and to move away from a position where they can do little other than ruthlessly attack their cost base in order to meet retailers' price demands. Brand owners want to outperform their rivals in terms of capturing market share, developing consumer and brand loyalty, and earning a rate of profit higher than the industry norm. Retailers, for their part, are seeking step changes that will reverse current trends, which have seen retail decline as a percentage of GDP over recent years. They need to find new and innovative ways to manage retail offerings in highly fragmented markets.

For both brand owners and retailers, a focus on innovation in value creation offers the most promising source of organic growth. This means working to create the next wave of brand and retail experiences, based on having a consumer-relevant value-centric orientation in the business, and a management culture that makes innovation possible.

Consumers as Innovators

In the production-driven economy, the role of the consumer in the innovation process was highly limited – so much so, in fact, that in some cases of marketing consumers appeared to be forgotten altogether. In the consumption-led economy, the active, knowledgeable and demanding New Consumer is the focal point of product and service innovation. Organizations that embrace New Consumer Marketing acknowledge this and believe that the consumer can be a source of insight and innovation leading to greater business competence. Such firms are characterized by high levels of consumer involvement; they recognize consumers as innovators.

The concept of using consumers in direct interface with business managers was termed 'Tapping the creativity of consumers'[TM] by the Synectics Corporation (www.synecticsworld.com), an international consultancy specializing in innovation and change. Synectics consultants engage consumers in the problem-solving process in the search for breakthrough initiatives. For example, one client, the National Farmers' Union (NFU), was brought together with consumers at the point of purchase, where it was observed that there was no easy way for consumers to identify the source of the food they were buying. This was an issue of serious concern in the UK following a number of high-profile food scares. The insight generated from speaking to grocery shoppers directly was that they wanted a convenient way to ensure food safety. This may seem an obvious requirement, but it led to the idea of a new farm-assurance branding scheme. The Farm Assured brand, authenticating how the food has been produced, hit the shelves within a record nine months, due to the involvement of all stakeholders (farmers, consumers, NFU staff, wholesalers and retailers).

By eliciting consumers' hidden desires and enabling them to participate fully in product development, organizations can use consumers as agents of change in the same way that a grit of sand can develop into a pearl within an oyster's shell. Cadbury Schweppes and Johnson Controls, companies working in diverse sectors, have both made maximum use of consumers to shape and sell products successfully.

Cadbury Schweppes

Cadbury Schweppes confectionery uses a five-stage process known as 'ALICE' to drive innovation in its Consumer Planning and Research Department. The acronym stands for: alignment (A) of the objectives of the research with the consumer problem, leverage (L) of existing knowledge within the business, immersion (I) in the world of the potential consumer, connection (C) through insight, and execution (E) to drive growth. The launch of the Boost Guarana chocolate bar in September 2002 followed this strategic development pathway. Its genesis was based on the insight that the highly demanding lifestyle of today's consumers takes a heavy toll on their mental energy. This learning was generated by a cross-functional team, and supported by desk research and consumer surveys that used a raft of ethnographic and direct questioning techniques. The stimulant properties of Boost Guarana match those of energy drinks that claim to deliver improved attention, alertness and concentration.

Source: Patsy Richardson, Head of Consumer Planning and Research, Cadbury Schweppes, 'How to maximise the benefits of using consumer insight to drive innovation', paper presented at the 'Using Consumer Insight for Profitable Innovation' Conference, IQPC, London, October 2002.

Johnson Controls

Johnson Controls is part of an automotive systems group that makes seats and car interiors. It operates in the business-to-business (B2B) sector as a supplier to well-known car manufacturers such as BMW and Nissan. The company believes that 'consumer focused innovation and product development will become an increasingly important competitive differentiator'. Recognizing that cars need to deliver more than 'just transportation' and that car interiors need to surprise and delight end users, Johnson Controls draws on the views of both automotive experts and car drivers to understand the motivating values of car drivers (e.g. family, safety, pragmatism, harmony). Consumers are consulted on product design and associated issues, such as what luxury means for car drivers and how drivers actually use the technology available in cars. This insight-turned-innovation is then used as a core competence by Johnson Controls in its relationships with its immediate customers, the car manufacturers.

Source: Jemina Martinez, Head of Advanced Consumer Research, Johnson Controls, 'Getting out of the car and into people's lives', paper presented at the 'Using Consumer Insight for Profitable Innovation' Conference, IQPC, London, October 2002.

Innovation through Process or People?

Many companies take an overtly process-oriented approach to managing innovation while others regard innovation as a capability vested in people. Managerial thinking is currently caught between these two contrasting approaches. How should an organization seeking to improve its performance by becoming more innovative achieve this? New Consumer Marketing offers a way of seeing these two approaches as part of the same solution to meeting the needs of New Consumers and providing breakthrough opportunities in business development for brand owners and retailers.

On the one hand, there is a clearly identified and well-used process that was formalized by Robert Cooper, an academic researcher, known as the stage–gate process (Cooper, 1993). This is shown in Figure 7.1. The stage–gate process provides a way of screening and monitoring the progression of projects to ensure that progress is linked to the successful achievement of business goals. It subdivides new product development activities into a series of stages so that managers can 'own' specific groups of activities and be responsible for achieving the objectives within those activities. In order to proceed from one stage to the next, the project must satisfy the objectives that were set for that stage. Failure at any stage in the process will result in the abandonment of the project. The definition of the developmental stages and the evaluation criteria will be specific to the organization concerned. The stage–gate process aims to reduce risk and is usually associated with an incremental approach to innovation.

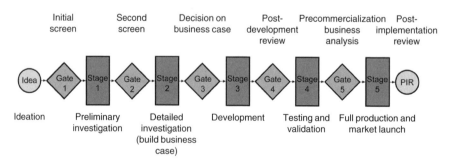

Figure 7.1 The stage–gate process. Adapted from Cooper (1993)

Cranfield School of Management 'Marketing Management: A relationship marketing perspective', 2000. Reproduced with permission of Palgrave Macmillan

On the other hand, there are many examples of organizations where innovation is directly attributable to the leadership and management style of an individual (usually the CEO), whose commitment to innovation is reflected in the culture of the organization. A common feature of these organizations is a focus on seeing things from the consumer's perspective. As a result they tend to be more effective in the marketplace. For example, Stelios Haji-Ioannou, founder of the low-cost carrier easyJet, used to take up to four flights a week on easyJet to experience what it was like as a passenger using his airline. The feedback and insight he gained from this unusual routine was used to improve consumer value.

Michael Dell,[1] founder and namesake of the world's leading computer services provider, says 'One of the challenges of a company that is succeeding is that you run the risk of complacency'. He encourages his team to explore incremental improvements and to experiment with ideas that add value, primarily in terms of efficiency. EasyJet and Dell demonstrate that fostering an innovative culture starts from the top: it is driven by the way that senior managers manage and relish risk, set challenging but measurable goals, support employees who take a risk in trying something different, champion new ideas, and encourage diversity of thought and approach.

Innovation as a Dynamic Capability

In order to synthesize this binary behaviour (seeking efficiency through process or effectiveness through people), New Consumer Marketing encourages a systemic approach. Drawing on learning from the living sciences, it helps in identifying the key underlying processes and relationships within the organization that enable it to become as adaptive and creative as possible in a changing market environment. This approach is exemplified by 3M(UK),[2] a company that continuously and consistently demonstrates success in innovation.

3M(UK)

The story of the 3M Post-it[TM], probably 3M's most well-known product, has become a classic example of innovation. 3M manager Art Fry sought a way of keeping the bookmark in his hymn book from slipping out onto the floor. He connected this desire to his knowledge of an adhesive that had been discovered by the company a number of years before, but discarded as it was considered to be ineffective at sticking. With the support of the company, Fry redeveloped the adhesive successfully and this led to the Post-it™, a hugely successful stationery innovation.

3M(UK) employees are given the freedom to take risks and try out new ideas, and this has led to a steady stream of new products. John Mueller, former Chairman and CEO of 3M(UK), is quoted as saying 'We want to institutionalize a bit of rebellion in our labs. It has been said that the competition never knows what we are going to come up with next. The fact is, neither do we'. This is indicative of a mindset that actively encourages radical innovation. The difference between this mindset and one that leads to incremental innovation is, so current research suggests (Dyck, 2002), to do with the way in which the organization experiences the complexity of the problem it is facing. Where an organization perceives the problem to be 'uncertain', it is essentially saying that it knows the variables at play but does not know how to configure them to find the solution. The organization that perceives the problem to be one of 'ambiguity' is going farther, and saying that it does not know what variables are at play and does not know the formula for solving the problem.

This latter attitude is reflected in Mueller's words and is associated with companies that seek to absorb complexity, rather than simply to reduce it. Organizations that work to reduce complexity are constrained to an incremental approach. Those whose starting point is that they do not know how to solve the problem can work to create options to develop potential solutions and in doing so, learn as an organization. Taking a broader view of the complexity of the marketplace and the issues facing consumers is less comfortable for organizations as it throws up more challenges and greater risk, but it can lead to more radical innovation where the rewards are potentially superior.

Therefore, managers seeking to improve organizational performance by becoming more innovative need to start by deciding whether they are uncertain or ambiguous about the complexity of the problem they are facing. Their answers will be based on their understanding of the marketplace and will determine whether they then work to reduce or absorb the complexity. This more reflective approach is not a capability that was called for in the production-driven era, where a command-and-control attitude dominated. Then, organizations produced goods and services and persuaded consumers to buy them. In today's consumption-led economy, where consumer markets are highly fragmented and changing fast, the successful players are those who are able to produce value in a consistent and cost-effective way. The market leaders, however, go one step further – they constantly seek to differentiate themselves from competitors by offering superior value in the form of new products and services. They are capable of absorbing complexity and mastering the organizational response to market change.

A Radical Approach to Innovation

Organizations can best distance themselves from the competition by changing the rules of the marketplace. This starts with generating insight into consumers' problems and expectations, and then defining them in such a way that creating the value consumers seek becomes obvious. As discussed in the previous chapter, this is the desired output of an effectively operating first cell in a demand system. To achieve value definition, the organization may well find itself redefining the consumer needs the industry is focusing on and thus contributing to industry understanding of the value-adding factors that matter to consumers. These might then form the basis of new performance criteria for companies in that sector. Those companies that fail to embrace the new criteria may risk losing out.

Virgin Group

Virgin Group is an organization that has demonstrated time and again how to bring radically new products and services into the marketplace without being the first to market in a particular sector. The company's understanding of the value-adding factors that matter to consumers has enabled it to successfully operate in markets where it has taken on established giants in a 'David versus Goliath' battle for consumer loyalty. For this reason, Virgin has gained a reputation as a challenger brand. For example, Virgin Mobile offered consumers a single, simple tariff when other operators were confronting consumers with an array of complicated tariffs. Virgin's uncomplicated approach won it 1.7 million customers by mid-2002 and catapulted the company into the position of the fifth largest mobile operator in the UK within three years of entering the market. Virgin Mobile's competitors have since copied the simple tariff system, effectively raising the key performance criteria for the industry.

Other Virgin businesses, such as Virgin Atlantic and Virgin One, have impacted their markets in a similar way. When Virgin Atlantic launched its

'Upper Class' seating, the idea of offering the large seats and legroom of traditional First Class for the price of a business class ticket was new, and won Virgin Atlantic a lucrative market share of key international routes. Virgin One again demonstrated the benefits of keeping it simple when it introduced the Virgin One bank account (now known as One), which enabled consumers to manage all their finances, including mortgages, savings and income, from a single account. The new type of bank account made its mark in an industry that had formerly offered consumers a range of banking products and where corporate emphasis was on persuading consumers to buy these products rather than developing products to suit consumer needs. Virgin's consistently simple and consumer-focused approach to innovation in value creation is indicative of a true value-orientation within the organization and also of a management culture that makes innovation possible.

Organizations such as Virgin Group take the consumer as their starting point and not the final destination for their products and services. They are less interested in simply building advantage over their competitors and rather keener on providing consumers with a step change in value that effectively creates a new market. The competition is left standing as old sources of advantage are destroyed and new ones are created.

W. Chan Kim and Renee Mauborgne, two professors from the French business school INSEAD, have published extensively in this area and they use the term 'value pioneers' to describe the Virgin Group and similar types of organization (1997, 1999a,b, 2000). These are businesses engaged in what Kim and Mauborgne define as 'value innovation', a process that makes the competition irrelevant and creates new markets by focusing on what value needs to be produced. They cite examples such as Callaway Golf, the US golf club manufacturer, which in 1991 launched its 'Big Bertha' golf club. The product rapidly rose to dominance, taking market share from rivals and expanding the total golf club market because its radically new design (the club has an unusually large head) offered players a way of overcoming the difficulties associated with hitting a small golf ball with a little golf club head. For Kim and Mauborgne, Callaway, like Charles Schwab & Co. in investment brokerage, IKEA in home products retail and Wal-Mart in discount retailing, illustrates their thesis that there is a clear link between high rates of business growth and a radical approach to innovation.

This stance contrasts with the traditional view that consumers can provide only limited help in innovative product and service development, as they are constrained by their experience and unable to articulate anything other than incremental ideas.

THE ROLE OF NEW PRODUCT DEVELOPMENT IN VALUE CREATION

There is a lot of debate around the question: how new does innovation really have to be? 'Newness' can be understood in a number of different ways. The word 'new' is often used in marketing communications, for example, in advertisements and mailings or on product packaging. However, in many instances consumers could be forgiven for asking what might actually be new about certain products or services. Newness is often defined by an incremental change to an existing product or service. It may be a barely discernible alteration to the pack size or ingredients base. Such a slight improvement in the value offering might make it 'new to the company but not new to the market'.

Alternatively, the newness element might be more extensive, to the point where consumers change their purchase behaviour. For example, when Mars launched its new Celebrations brand, the Roses and Quality Street brands already dominated the marketplace for boxed, wrapped chocolates for everyday occasions. But Mars had undertaken in-depth research into potential consumers and used the resulting insight to position the new brand as 'all your favourite countline products in miniature'. The launch of Celebrations succeeded in attracting a younger consumer compared to rival brands, and Mars captured a significant share of the UK's £600 million boxed chocolate market within a short period of time.

In essence, product newness is a spectrum carrying increasing amounts of business risk for the organization. In their report *New Product Management for the 1980s*, Booz, Allen & Hamilton (1982) provide a way of looking at innovation in terms of product newness. They identify six categories of new product development as defined by the product's level of newness to the firm and its perceived level of newness to consumers. Their grid displaying the various categories is shown in Figure 7.2.

It is evident from Figure 7.2 that the new product developments with lowest risk are those created through cost reduction and brand repositioning. Cost reduction involves the organization in paring down the

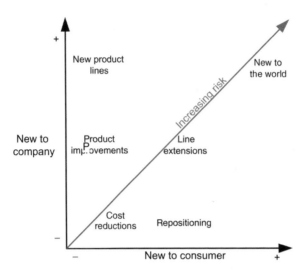

Figure 7.2 Categories of new product development. Adapted from Booz, Allen & Hamilton (1982)

Reprinted by permission of Pearson Education for the work written by Simon Knox, Adrian Payne, Martin Christopher, Malcolm Mcdonald entitled 'Creating a Company for Customers'

content of the value proposition by a specific amount to save on cost. Where the reduction is minimal, it may not affect consumer perceptions of value. However, excessive cost reduction or too many small reductions over time does become noticeable. Brand repositioning represents relatively higher risk as it usually involves presenting brand revisions of some form to the consumer. The organization may or may not succeed at realigning the brand with consumer expectations, but it is already familiar with managing the brand.

New product developments that carry intermediate risk include line extensions and product improvements. The usual strategy here is to enhance consumer value by increasing product choice and product performance respectively. For example, Müller, the fourth largest grocery brand in the UK, has consistently increased the range of yoghurt varieties to more than 20 in order to drive sales volume and market share. A number of other food brands have chosen to focus instead on product performance and have altered their recipes to include added vitamins and fibre, thus moving their brands into the functional foods, or 'nutraceuticals', sector of the market.

The highest risk new product developments are ones that are both new to the company and new to consumers. These are known as 'new-to-the-world' introductions. The annals of marketing are littered with examples of unsuccessful new-to-the-world products, such as Betamax videotape and Clive Sinclair's C5 electric car. These new products failed to deliver any substantial consumer benefit and were therefore not adopted by consumers. These attempts at innovation were not anchored in any form of meaningful consumer insight.

Many organizations mistakenly believe that adding more technology to a product or service will result in value-adding innovation. However, what consumers want from technology is new or enhanced value that will extend their abilities and provide them with greater ease of use and convenience. Successful new-to-the-world innovation succeeds because it represents a genuine breakthrough in delivering a value proposition based on a deep understanding of the nature of the value consumers seek. This new-to-the-world form of innovation is also known as radical, or discontinuous, innovation, as referred to earlier. The introduction of Mars Ice Cream is an example of this type of approach.

Mars Ice Cream

In the late 1980s, ice cream was a price-sensitive, seasonal commodity. The market was large (£587 million) but stagnant, and dominated by Walls and Lyons Maid, which held 45% and 14% market share, respectively. Most ice cream was vegetable-fat based and generally came in the form of ice-lollies, cones and family brick packs. Until Mars entered the market in 1988, ice cream was viewed largely as a children's snack and demographics showed it could be a shrinking market. However, Mars identified a gap in the existing market for a premium-price, branded ice cream. It was the first to launch such a product and gained a lead over other ice cream manufacturers. The new product was sold in the same outlets that stocked the existing range of Mars confectionery, enabling the company to use the same sales force and existing resources. This allowed significant economies, and lessened the financial burden of entering a new market.

THE ROLE OF BRANDING IN VALUE CREATION

Brands play an important role in the value-creation process, and the changing marketing landscape, created by the shift from a production-driven to a consumption-led economy, has already brought forth new thinking about them and their meaning for consumers. Initially, brands emerged as a simple means of identifying the manufacturer of a product.

For example, in 1266, in medieval England, bakers were required by law to put their mark on every loaf of bread sold so that if there were any discrepancies in weight the baker at fault could be traced. The practice of branding a product with an 'identity' has continued and developed. Today, the brand concept is highly complex, having evolved beyond the core product to include various kinds of added value. Brands are often depicted as a 'fried egg', with a functional centre surrounded by layers of less tangible elements such as reputation, pack design, advertising, guarantees, and so on. This view of brands typified the approach of marketers in the 1950s and 1960s, when brands were seen as 'lifeless, manipulable artefacts' (Hanby, 1999) and consumers were seen as passive purchasers.

Brand thinking moved ahead slowly until the early 1980s, when researcher Judie Lannon and psychologist Peter Cooper (1983) expressed the idea that 'what turns a product into a brand is that the physical product is combined with something else – symbols, images, feelings – to produce an idea which is more than the sum of the parts. The two – product and symbolism – live and grow with and on one another in a partnership of mutual exchange'. This concept began a process of seeing the brand not just as the producer's idea of the product, but also as the consumer's idea of the product, giving rise to the notion of brands being co-created by producers together with consumers.

By the mid-1990s the nature of the intangible value inherent in the brand had evolved to the extent that Harvard professor Susan Fournier (1996) described consumers' relationships with mass brands as able to 'soothe the "empty selves" left behind by society's abandonment of tradition and community and provide stable anchors in an otherwise changing world'. At the close of the twentieth century, John Grant, author of the influential *New Marketing Manifesto* (1999), observed that 'Brands seem to have taken on a life of their own. They have become quite freestanding ideas that take hold and spread. So that Virgin can span many markets, and Viagra can become a potent icon, even in markets where it is not yet available. ... A brand is a popular idea or set of ideas that people live by'.

These quotations by leading marketing commentators demonstrate the changing way in which brands are believed to operate. Today, the metaphors used to describe the brand-building process are no longer mechanistic but organic in nature, in keeping with the discipline of New Consumer Marketing. Brands are now thought of as living entities that take on a life of their own inside consumers' minds, creating something known as a 'mental model'. Mental models, as described in the previous chapter, provide insight into how consumers create, store, recall and relate to brands in everyday life. In effect, a brand becomes a representation of an individual's collection of experiences at each of the 'touchpoints' at which the brand wittingly or unwittingly engages the consumer. These experiences provide a mix of rational, emotional, social and cultural benefits to the individual consumer. If the supplying organization is defining and creating value effectively, then this bundle of complementary benefits will be delivered through the value-adding factors associated with the brand. A brand is, therefore, the consumer's experience of the value proposition.

Brands exist because people want them to exist. As Niall Fitzgerald, Chairman of Unilever, commented, 'Even if the word "marketing" had never been invented and advertising was banned across the globe, there would still be brands, because it is people who need them'.[3] For consumers, brands provide a way of making a complicated world simpler. Consumers become so familiar with them that brands provide a shorthand approach to decision making. The dependable predisposition of consumers to purchase specific brands provides brand owners with assets that offer the promise of future cash flow. It is consumers, then, and not companies, who invest a brand with its value.

If this is the case, how is it that brands go into decline and die? The answer is that companies kill them, though not always deliberately or knowingly. The decline and death of a brand can occur in a number of different ways; for example, through organizational arrogance, greed or complacency. Underlying this ebbing away of brand value is the absence of a value-centric orientation in the organization. A value-centric orientation enables the company to know, understand and anticipate the value consumers are seeking so that it can then focus its value-producing resources on satisfying those needs, thereby ensuring that brands survive. The Barbie doll is one such example.

Barbie

Barbie began as an innovation and has remained relevant to young girls throughout the doll's 40-year history. The Barbie doll was created in 1959 and over 1 billion Barbies have been sold to date. The brand is worth some $2 billion, making it the most valuable toy brand in the world. Mattel, the

American toy giant that manufactures the doll, claims the average American girl aged between 3 and 11 owns ten Barbies.

When Barbie burst onto the scene in the 1960s the doll market consisted mainly of baby dolls, designed for girls to cradle, rock and feed. In contrast, Barbie had adult features and represented an independent young woman. Since Barbie's launch as a teenage fashion model, Mattel has worked to keep the doll's image fresh and to deliver the play value its ever-younger consumers demand. Every year the company devises about 150 different Barbie dolls, and designs some 120 new doll outfits. Barbie's image is constantly updated, mirroring the changing role of women in society. She now comes in a multiplicity of guises, from astronaut to army officer to dentist and many more. To reflect the growing diversity of populations, African American, Hispanic and Asian variations were introduced as early as the 1960s.

Barbie has survived the challenges of 'age compression', or kids getting 'older' at a younger age. Girls now grow out of traditional play patterns, including playing with dolls, earlier than they did in the past. Whereas a generation ago 12-year-olds might have played with Barbie, today's prime audience is aged three to five. Mattel is meeting this challenge head on by introducing extensions to the Barbie brand. For example, *Barbie in the Nutcracker* is a computer-animated video that has generated $150 million from sales. The company is dedicated to promoting Barbie as a lifestyle, not just a toy. In addition to selling the dolls, Mattel licenses Barbie in 30 different product categories, from furniture to make-up. A girl can sleep in Barbie pyjamas, under a Barbie duvet-cover, in a bedroom covered in Barbie wallpaper. There are even Barbie conventions, fan clubs, websites, magazines and collectors' events. To many commentators, Barbie transcends the product category and is an icon, representing 'the face of the American dream'.

Source: 'Life in Plastic', *The Economist*, 21 December, 2002.

Building Successful Brands

As the meaning of brands has shifted over time, so too has organizational understanding of how to build brands. In the production-driven era it was believed that brand building was best achieved solely through marketing communications activities (namely advertising). Brand development was seen as the transmission of messages to consumers, the aim being to control their purchase behaviour. Today, brands are built on a much wider platform that may, for example, involve alliance partners or staff.

... through alliances – i-mode

i-mode is the most successful mobile data service in the world to date. Since its launch in Japan in February 1999, i-mode has attracted 35.3 million subscribers (58% of market share), who each pay on average ¥1,540 per month for services encompassing 3,290 official and 59,869 unofficial content sites. This success has been achieved through a value-centric approach to the development, implementation and operation of i-mode services. By keeping its offer simple, maintaining effective content development and being first to market, i-mode has gained significant competitive advantage and become the object of envy among mobile operators worldwide.

Domoco, the company behind the i-mode brand, whose name is derived from 'do communications over the mobile', has worked to define and satisfy consumers' needs through a relevant and appealing brand by forging alliances with leading content providers. The brand is based on the understanding that compelling entertainment content drives demand and the technological aspects consequently take a back seat. As Takeshi Natsuno, director of i-mode's strategy department, explains, 'We never emphasize words such as internet, web browsing and mobile computing to consumers. i-mode users can get various information only with simple operations without recognizing they are using the internet'.

Putting this philosophy into practice, Domoco carefully selects and controls 'official' partner sites on the basis of freshness, reliability, depth of content and clear user benefit, and provides them with key services such as user verification, joint marketing and technical assistance. The technological capabilities of i-mode allow content providers to charge users small incremental fees for the services provided. These fees are billed by Domoco and then passed on to the content provider, but Domoco retains a 9% commission. This business model creates a positive feedback loop whereby good content and compelling services attract fee-paying users, who in turn attract more content providers. For example, games manufacturer Badai provides a new animated character every day as i-mode screen wallpaper (the background screen image for i-mode). With over 2 million i-mode users signing up for the service at ¥100 per month, this strategic alliance nets the company more than £13 million per annum, proving the strength of a partnership approach. Similar agreements have been made with Sony, allowing it to provide Playstation style games over i-mode, and Coca-Cola, whereby i-mode users can use their handsets to pay for and acquire items from individual Coca-Cola vending machines.

... through staff – Singapore Airlines

Some companies are distinguished in their marketplace by the level of service they offer. The way in which their employees deal with consumers becomes the defining characteristic of the brand. In essence, the staff are the brand. With a proven profitability record over 30 years, Singapore Airlines is one of the most successful airlines in the world and is consistently used by travellers and competitors as a benchmark for outstanding performance. Key to this success has been the delivery of the brand through the airline's staff.

The Singapore Airlines brand is intrinsically linked with the Singapore Girl, launched in 1972, whose serene face has become the heart of the carrier's advertising campaign. No other airline has such a strong brand image, one that has even been immortalized in wax at Madame Tussaud's Museum in London. Ian Batey, the creator of the Singapore Girl, took a risk when he proposed that adverts should focus on service at a time when other airlines were selling their tickets on the theme of safety. Batey attributes the success of the brand to its 'combination of silk and steel ... the ever-changing, cutting-edge, body side of the brand ... and the softer soul side. Together, you have a certain Asian humility, graciousness and warmth as well as being extremely fit, fast, modern and contemporary'. The airline operates with a ratio of one flight attendant for every 22 passengers, the highest in the world and well above the industry average.

Singapore Airlines has more than 14,000 staff located in cities throughout the world. People from different cultures must work together to produce a seamless and positive customer experience. To unite the diverse and geographically separated workforce, the airline has developed a number of activities to encourage inter-office communication, including a variety of department newsletters and a monthly company-wide internal magazine. A 'Staff Ideas in Action' scheme ensures that new suggestions are constantly put forward. The results of these and many other efforts add up to a staff culture that is vigorously committed to the airline, to consumers and to continuous improvement. Staff pride and sense of ownership are evident in the way employees work to uphold the airline's reputation, which is built on a well-defined set of corporate values.

Emerging Brand Issues

An emerging issue for brand owners and retailers in today's consumption-led economy is the growing debate about the impact of globalization and the role of business versus government. While this may not appear to be linked to the value-creation process in any obvious way, it represents a breaking trend that needs to be monitored for its impact on the kind of value that consumers seek and may be seeking in future. Brands are increasingly the targets of anti-corporation campaigns, as is evidenced in the protests against the World Trade Organization (WTO) in Seattle and Genoa, and the boycotting of genetically modified (GM) foods. In some cases, consumer behaviour towards certain brands has been shown to be a more effective political weapon than the ballot box. Shell, for example, found itself at the centre of controversy in 1995 when it sought to dispose of the Brent Spar oil platform at sea. Consumers expressed their concern for the environment by not buying Shell petrol, especially in Germany where Shell sales declined by 50% on one day.

Although these brand issues may seem far removed from their day-to-day remit, marketers need to develop some sort of perspective on them. In several cases, the monetary value of the value-creation activities of some corporations exceeds that of a number of nation states. An acknowledged authority in this area is socio-economist Dr Noreena Hertz. She explains in her book *The Silent Takeover* (2001) how corporations are changing people's lives, society and the democratic process. She points out that of the world's 100 largest economies, 51 are now corporations and only 49 are nation states. Combined sales at General Motors and Ford are greater than the GDP of the whole of sub-Saharan Africa, and Wal-Mart now has a turnover higher than the revenues of most states of Eastern Europe.

At the heart of the debate about growing globalization and the role of business versus government lies the issue of trust: is consumer marketing acting as a trustworthy agent in the economic system? Brands are involved in the economy and the production of national wealth because, as discussed earlier, they act as a label of guarantee and trust for consumers and this value-enhancing aspect still plays a major role in motivating purchases today. A small but demanding minority of New Consumers wants to make informed purchasing decisions and they have a growing interest in the company behind the brand. Their concerns focus on wider societal issues such as environmental vulnerability, poverty, and economic and political instability, and they have a desire to link their purchasing habits with the future of sustainable development. This represents a significant change in the kind of value that consumers want and challenges traditional value-creation activities.

This wider agenda brings to the fore company reputation. Brand owners have always known that strong brands invite, earn, honour and reward the trust of consumers but the signs are that to be a strong brand in the new marketplace, a brand has to demonstrate some form of corporate social responsibility. The response of business has, however, been limited. While most companies are still trying to understand exactly how this trend impacts the value creation process, Body Shop is an example of a company that has embraced brand ethics from its inception. For many consumers, Body Shop is not simply a retailer but a cause worth supporting. Body Shop's promotion of 'beauty without cruelty to animals' and 'trade not aid' positions the brand as environmentally and socially responsible. Other companies have developed social responsibility programmes as a means of achieving profitability for their business and the environment in a way that reflects the values of society. Reputation management cannot, however, simply be regarded as a tactical activity. Companies have to find ways of embedding social responsibility into their organizations. As researcher Lance Moir (2001) comments, 'The best firms in this area – such as BP, Shell, Johnson & Johnson – are looking at their business processes in order to ensure that the pure economic motive is not the sole determinant of business decisions'.

THE ROLE OF POSITIONING IN VALUE CREATION

The positioning of a brand in the marketplace is a manifestation of where it sits vis-à-vis the competition, and in the same way that consumers invest a brand with its value, they also determine the positioning of a brand. Just as they carry in their minds a mental model of an individual brand, they also carry a mental map of related brands. Knowledge of this can reveal to the organization the competitive set within which it operates. The challenge facing the insight generators in a business is to find the right combination of tools and techniques to uncover these maps. (These issues were discussed in Chapter 6.) However, having generated this knowledge, the organization can then work to create the value proposition, and ultimately, to deliver it. Positioning plays an important role in the value creation process because it helps build and sustain the value proposition. Moreover, it does so in a way that factors in emotion, the great intangible aspect of brand building.

An example of a positioning map is shown in Figure 7.3. It shows the key criteria that consumers use to discriminate between branded concepts in the eating out market: in this case, the type of food on offer and the atmosphere of the outlet. Consumers will then go on to opt for a 'French' brasserie versus a 'department store' cafeteria depending on the type of eating-out occasion they are planning. For example, they may be contemplating a meal out with a small group of friends to celebrate a special occasion, or they may be thinking of somewhere to go on their own to pick up a snack as they are in a hurry. New Consumers are ultra discriminating and value creation should focus on their perceptions of value, which here includes type of outlet, speed of service, ambience, etc.

Drawing out the Emotional Message

New Consumers are motivated by the desire for experiences over features and benefits, and the brand positioning process provides an important way of linking an emotional message to the physical characteristics of the brand. Brands touch people's lives, and consumers choose brands for the emotional values they express as much as anything else. The more deeply embedded the emotions are, the more strongly the consumer is connected to the brand. The example of Nike trainers given in Chapter 6 showed how particular product features delivered certain benefits, which together provided an experience that satisfied a higher-level value requirement.

Similar research[4] carried out on purchasers of women's fine fragrances shows in more detail how perceived value delivers an experience for consumers. The study illustrates how certain features of a brand of perfume, in this instance Chanel No. 5, are linked with specific perceived benefits that satisfy personal values. It can be seen from Figure 7.4 how the brand's country of origin (France) works as a positive feature, providing reassurance to consumers. Consumers regard Chanel No. 5 as a low-risk, high-quality purchase because of the trustworthy reputation French

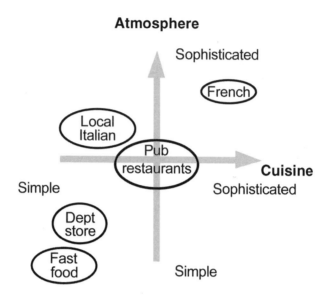

Figure 7.3 A positioning map of the UK eating-out market

perfumes have in the marketplace. This feeling of reassurance promotes a sense of well-being and feeling good about oneself. For Chanel, the learning to be drawn from this is that it is important to retain the 'Frenchness' of the brand, as it is integral to the brand's positioning and communications strategies.

These insights linking the physical attributes of the brand to the emotional benefits they deliver and, in some cases, to the higher-level personal values that are satisfied through ownership, can enable brand owners to be more innovative in their positioning strategies. Certain brand owners explicitly use these sorts of insights to drive their value-creation processes. For example, motorbike manufacturer Harley-Davidson builds on the idea of ownership conferring a particular way of life. From the bikes to the merchandise to the tattoos, consumers see Harley-Davidson as a part of their identity, enabling the brand to strongly differentiate itself in the marketplace. In the personal computer (PC) sector, the iMAC is positioned as a sensual product, infused with mystery, thereby engendering a warmth for the brand among consumers. For consumers of these brands, the emotional switching costs are significant. For the organizations behind the brands, their brand positioning is the result of an ongoing strategic process

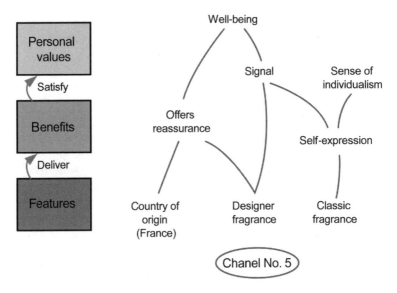

Figure 7.4 Mapping brand linkages

that informs the creation and delivery of the value proposition. It is not the result of an ad hoc tactical communications campaign.

The Positioning Process

To guide the efforts of an organization in the positioning process, it is usual to create a simple statement of what the brand is about and how the communications strategy should support its market positioning. For most organizations, the ease with which this statement is created is directly correlated with the way the positioning process is managed. As Sergio Zyman, former advertising VP at Coca-Cola, once said, 'If you want to establish a clear image in the minds of consumers, you first need a clear image in your own mind'. However, this is seldom achieved, for a number of different reasons. For instance, some organizations seek to include everything in the positioning statement, attempting to be all things to all people. Others do not know where to start the process of articulation. Yet others insist on allowing everyone in the organization to have an opinion and try to reflect them all in a concise statement. This process needs to be driven by someone who has clear responsibility for the task, resulting in an unambiguous brand positioning. In addition, the adoption of a simple approach (where less is more), and the ability to take a long-term view aid the successful completion of the task. Burberry exemplifies the ability of an organization to achieve a turnaround in fortunes based on a firmly managed repositioning process.

Burberry

In recent years Burberry has repositioned itself successfully by redefining the value consumers are seeking and creating an improved value proposition for them. In the mid-1990s, Burberry's unique British heritage and famous trademark – the red, black, camel and white check pattern – was no longer enough to save the dysfunctional retailer. Burberry had become over-reliant on tired products and by 1997 trading profit collapsed. In October 1997, Rose Marie Bravo took over as CEO and began a process of repositioning the brand, propelling it into luxury status. Her aim was to turn the staid British brand that was being eclipsed by competitors into an iconic and aspirational brand with cross-generational appeal. By February 1999, Burberry was a firm favourite on the catwalks of Milan. Burberry designs, ranging from the classic trench coat to funky pink kilts, fuelled an explosion of accessories also in the trademark check. Since 1998, Burberry sales have doubled and the brand is now seen as a financial success.

The repositioning of Burberry was achieved by having a clear vision in place. Bravo recognized that although Burberry had become stale, the public

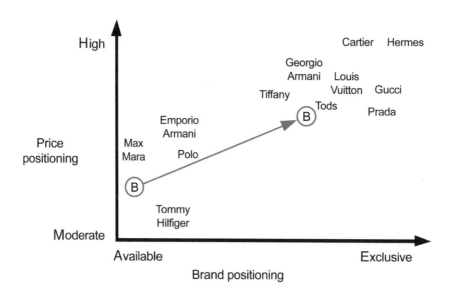

Figure 7.5 Repositioning Burberry

still associated strongly with its heritage and quality. Under her guidance the company began to reposition itself as the authentic British lifestyle brand. This moved it into competition with high-margin luxury design houses such as Gucci, Prada and Ralph Lauren, with the opportunity for superior returns (see Figure 7.5).

Burberry's remarkable recovery was achieved through repositioning the brand, changing and expanding the product mix, and changing the structure of distribution and sales channels. Concentrating on the repositioning of the brand, Burberry retained its four core values (quality, classic, heritage, iconic) and adopted four more (innovation, style, aspiration, modernity) in order to create a modern spin to widen its appeal and raise global recognition. A key success factor was a coherent communications strategy across all media, orchestrated to deliver a consistent image worldwide. Leading models, such as Stella Tenant and Kate Moss, were used to inspire more fashion-oriented advertising. Product design was improved with the input of Roberto Menichetti and then, in 2001, Christopher Bailey, as chief designer. Sponsorship of high-profile events such as the Mario Testino Exhibition at the National Portrait Gallery and the Burberry Cup, a polo match in association with the Prince of Wales, reinforced the brand's high class, British pedigree.

Other activities reinforced the brand's revitalized position. For example, the product mix was expanded to include high-margin accessories, childrenswear, and a perfume. The range of men's and women's apparel was consolidated, distribution was reviewed and retail channels were rationalized. As a part of this process, a large number of product licences were terminated as they were judged to be inconsistent with the repositioned brand image.

THE ROLE OF PRICE IN VALUE CREATION

Price plays a key role in the value-creation process. It can, for example, indicate value and quality. In the case of a Rolex watch or a Pret A Manger sandwich, the premium price reflects the 'premiumness' of the brand. Similarly, price can be used to support brand positioning: Stella Artois is advertised as a 'reassuringly expensive' lager and easyJet occupies a well-defined, value-for-money niche in the air travel market. In other words, price works in combination with other elements of the marketing mix as a signal of value for consumers.

Consumer goods companies are coming under increasing pressure to review their pricing strategies as both consumers and trade customers sharpen their focus on value, aided in many cases by the power of the Internet in their search for best value. The introduction of the Euro and changing European legislation have added to pricing complexity. When setting pricing strategies, it is important for managers to understand the role that price plays in the value proposition. Price is used by consumers as a criterion for evaluating the value of the offer and by supplying organizations as a competitive tool. The effect of the shift from a production-driven to a consumption-led economy has forced many organizations to replace their cost-plus approach to pricing with demand-led pricing policies.

For brand owners, price is a significant lever in ensuring that value is defined, created and delivered at a profit. Revenue is, after all, the outcome of volume multiplied by price (and volume itself is impacted by price). Increases in profitability can be gained by increasing prices, reducing costs, or increasing the volume sold. However, it is changes in price levels that have the biggest impact on profitability due to the gearing ratio, which means that a greater amount of the benefit will flow through to the bottom line compared to the other two strategies. Volume increases are countered by variable costs, and reducing costs usually applies to values significantly smaller than turnover.

Brand owners must take account of a number of factors when drawing up a pricing plan. As depicted in Figure 7.6, these include internal costs, targets and constraints, pricing strategy (to be premium or not), competitor pricing strategy, and consumer insight. The outputs of this pricing decision-making process will impact the business case, and influence how performance monitoring and scenario planning are undertaken. Current pricing is often driven by past events rather than logic and consistency, leading to a situation where pricing is inconsistent across markets. For example, prices may be set by individual countries or by corporate divisions acting in isolation from the rest of the organization. A single company may use several different approaches to pricing in order to respond to short-term or local market needs or it may be that different prices have been agreed as part of key account management negotiations.

The Evaluation of Value

It is not uncommon for prices to be set without reference to the consumer's evaluation of the value proposition, leading to a situation where consumers

Figure 7.6 The complex pricing decision-making process. Adapted from Marketing Improvements, 2002

Reproduced by permission of RSM Marketing Improvements Ltd

believe price is out of line; that is, too expensive or even too cheap. This incomplete approach to pricing can also undermine brand-positioning strategies and may potentially damage the brand. Furthermore, it can lead to a situation where parallel trading develops, leading to lost profit opportunities. The way to prevent these issues arising is to base pricing strategy on a rigorous analysis of all the elements inherent in complex price decision making. Pricing strategy must take account of both the consumer's and the organization's evaluation of value, as shown in Figure 7.7. Clearly, each player makes a trade-off in the value exchange. Brand owners bear the costs of defining, creating and delivering value and need a healthy profit margin to remain in business while consumers incur costs associated with evaluating the value proposition and gaining ownership of the brand.

Consumers tend to evaluate the value proposition not in terms of the ticket price but in terms of relative value; that is, whether the offer seems expensive, cheap or fair to them. This notion is not new. Price as a reflection of the value placed on a product or service by the consumer was an idea first articulated by the Victorian economist Alfred Marshall. His beliefs about the effects of consumer preferences on transactions dominated economic

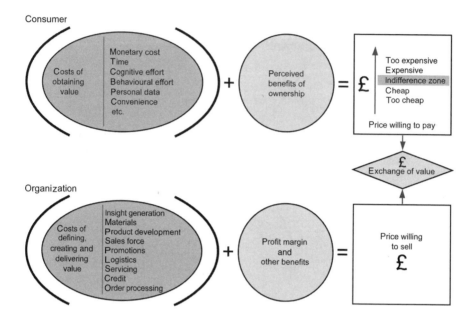

Figure 7.7 The evaluation of value

thinking until the middle of the twentieth century. The concept of the rational consumer, or 'homo economicus', held sway until the 1950s, when the idea that product attributes other than price might be influencing the purchase decision was promulgated. It was suggested that price might have more than one meaning for consumers. At about the same time, the idea of psychological price emerged. The underlying assumption here is that price has a double meaning for consumers. Besides the maximum price that they would be willing to pay, it is believed that there is also a minimum price for the product to be credible. In other words, consumers have an upper and a lower price limit in mind.

This concept has been refined through further research, and pricing theorists now talk about consumers' 'indifference zone'. The boundaries of this psychological zone are marked by a belief that, at the upper limit, if something is too expensive, then consumers will not buy it because they feel the price is unjustified, while at the lower limit, if something is too cheap, they will not buy it because they feel the value is suspect. Uncovering this indifference zone can form the basis of a successful demand-led pricing strategy, in line with the tenets of the New Consumer

Marketing model. Ryanair is one example of an organization that takes this value-centric approach to pricing seriously.

Ryanair

Ryanair is now the most valuable and profitable airline in Europe. It has powered its way to success by identifying a large, under-served customer base: the leisure traveller. Ryanair segmented the travel market and, on recognizing that the key values of the leisure traveller are price and punctuality, implemented a strategy to deliver low prices and on-time flights. In doing so, the company evolved a successful low-yield/high-volume business model.

Ryanair created its value proposition to appeal to the price-conscious consumer by choosing to compete on routes served by large, full-price carriers, such as Air France and Lufthansa. These airlines are highly subsidized and therefore have little incentive to reduce their operating costs, keeping prices to consumers high. By removing non-value-added items such as meals, assigned seating and the use of major airports, Ryanair was able to offer prices up to 80–90% lower than the flag carriers on numerous routes. As a result, it was able to gain market share and brand recognition within each route market. Ryanair's low cost base also forms a significant barrier to competition from larger airlines with high fixed costs.

Taking advantage of the deregulation of the European market and the growing demand for affordable and reliable air travel, Ryanair has created a brand experience that delivers more for less. Pricing is managed in real time. Flights booked months ahead of departure are made available at the lowest prices while those booked nearer to the travel date are more expensive. To keep processing costs down, consumers are also encouraged, using financial inducements, to book via the airline's website rather than over the phone.

This second cell of the New Consumer Marketing model is an essential building block in a demand system. It enables the organization to move from defining value to creating and communicating that value effectively, and eventually to delivering it. While the process of value creation is dependent on the interplay of new product development, branding, positioning and pricing, it is ultimately the role of innovation that underpins its success.

SUMMARY POINTS

- Innovation provides a way of creating new value-producing resources, or endowing existing ones with an enhanced potential for yielding profit.

- It is the consumer, and not the competition, that lies at the heart of innovation. Providing consumers with a step change in value that effectively creates a new market can leave the competition standing as old sources of advantage are destroyed and new ones created.

- Organizations that work to reduce marketplace complexity are constrained to an incremental approach to innovation. Those that choose to absorb it can then work to create options and learn as an organization, resulting in more radical forms of innovation.

- Brands have become the consumer's experience of the value proposition.

- Brands are no longer built just through advertising to consumers; they utilize other stakeholders, including alliances and staff.

- The positioning of a brand in the marketplace is a manifestation of where it sits vis-à-vis the competition, and in the same way that consumers invest a brand with its value, they also determine the positioning of a brand.

- Price represents the evaluation of the value proposition, and the effect of the shift from a production-driven to a consumption-led economy is forcing organizations to switch their strategy from a cost-plus approach to demand-led pricing policies.

Value Delivery 8

The process of delivering value to a specified audience through the media and channels of their choice:

- Delivering value = communicating and distributing the value created
- Watchword = agility

In the consumption-led economy, value delivery is undergoing rapid change for two important reasons: the emergence of the New Consumer and the proliferation of media and channels. This changing marketing environment poses new challenges for organizations, particularly in respect to how they manage media and channel choices, customer service and the supply chain. To be effective, organizations must ensure that their strategies for each of these key areas are aligned with the overall strategy of their demand system. As with the first two cells, this means having a value-centric orientation in the business.

Value delivery is concerned with how consumers get to own the product or service. It involves the way in which the offer is presented, the transaction is handled, and after-sales service and support are provided. The third cell of the New Consumer model focuses on communicating and distributing value in order to achieve maximum consumer responsiveness and satisfaction. The key to success here is organizational agility.

THE ROLE OF AGILITY IN VALUE DELIVERY

For a company to be agile, it is to be capable of operating profitably in a customer environment of continually, and unpredictable, changing customer opportunities.

(S. Goldman et al., 1995)

In the new marketplace of proliferating media and channel choices, characterized by an increasing number of new products and services, and a decline in organizational ability to forecast sales, organizations need to be able to respond rapidly and flexibly to consumer requirements. This demands a capability to change gear and immerse the organization in new opportunities on a continual basis. The phrase that resonates with managers is 'the need to develop organizational agility'.

The notion of organizational agility has its origins in flexible manufacturing systems, where it was believed that automation alone would confer this capability. Over time, a wider business application has emerged, largely through developments in supply-chain management. Current thinking defines organizational agility as 'a business-wide capability that embraces organizational structures, information systems, logistics processes and, in particular, mindsets'.[1] The agile organization creates competitive advantage for itself by being able to adapt its people and processes to the continually changing needs of the marketplace, increasingly with the support of technical innovation. The challenge for consumer-serving companies is to fuse people and process approaches in order to achieve cost-effective value delivery. Competitive advantage today lies in recruiting and motivating the right people, while at the same time constantly improving business processes. When either element, people or process, fails to embrace change, the organization is less nimble and thus less able to compete successfully.

Organizational culture plays a significant role in achieving and maintaining such agility. The fusion of people and processes can only take place in an environment conducive to effective change management. Creating an appropriate organizational culture involves a number of factors, including, for example, the management of employees, the sharing of knowledge and the choice of performance indicators. These factors are considered in more depth in the next chapter, but are raised here as they can be seen to have an impact on organizational agility in the cases offered in this chapter.

New Consumer Marketing promotes organizational agility by encouraging a value-centric orientation in the organization. A business that is focused on defining, creating and delivering value profitably is a business that can 'turn on a sixpence' and exploit opportunities.

The Veterans Agency (VA), formerly known as the War Pensions Agency, provides a useful example.

The Veterans Agency

The Veterans Agency (VA) is responsible for assessing and paying pensions to disabled servicemen and women and their spouses in the UK. It was established in Elizabethan times (when soldiers were paid £10 a year), but was launched as an executive agency in the mid-1990s. In November 2000, when the UK Prime Minister Tony Blair announced that surviving former prisoners of war in the Far East were to receive a £10,000 special payment from the Government, the VA was faced with the task of tracking down thousands of individuals dispersed across the world. As an agile organization, one that had its people and processes focused on consumer responsiveness, its project plan enabled 14,000 claims to be processed in less than three months.

For many organizations, adopting a market-responsive approach to value delivery is a daily challenge. Building on organizational strengths, segmenting customers in a meaningful way and utilizing IT to meet specific objectives are a few of the many ways in which organizations can improve their flexibility and customer responsiveness. Lastminute.com is a good example here.

Lastminute.com

In 2001, the web-based travel company handled some 800,000 online transactions, which included travel, hotel and restaurant bookings, and gift purchases. Around 20% of the £124 million transaction value was generated outside its key markets in the UK and France. Lastminute constantly redesigns its website (see Figure 8.1), brings in new suppliers and improves the customer experience. Its investment in IT is high due to a concentration on web design, connectivity, voice-recognition software and a sophisticated CRM system that segments 5 million customers on a database according to their purchasing habits. The CRM system enables Lastminute to email special offers to selected customers, based on the company's knowledge of their previous purchases. Since its launch four years ago, the company has grown quickly through the acquisition of rivals and the involvement of major players (e.g. BAA, Sony Music, Deutsche Telekom, France Telecom and Intel), who have bought equity stakes in the company.

THE ROLE OF MEDIA AND CHANNELS IN VALUE DELIVERY

New Consumers live in a global marketplace where they are increasingly offered lower prices, greater convenience and more choice. This is in large

Figure 8.1 Lastminute.com
Last Minute Network Ltd 2003

part due to the proliferation of media and channels which organizations use to market their brands, products and services. Media strategies have to do with how the value proposition is *communicated*, while channel strategies have to do with how it is *transacted*. The role of media and channels is of vital importance in delivering the value proposition as it relates to how and where the exchange of value takes place. With today's empowered consumers, able to go to market more easily than ever before, organizations can no longer afford to manage media and channels as if they were stand-alone entities.

In the production-driven era, media and channels were distinguishable from one another. For instance, television was considered a medium and retail was considered a channel. Now, in the consumption-led economy, media and channels have become closely related and even interchangeable. For example, the retailer is rapidly becoming the media owner's biggest competitor. This is evident in the fact that the 'big four' food retailers – Tesco, Asda, Safeway and Sainsbury's – currently account for 70% of household food expenditure, and the media issue facing brand owners is whether to advertise on television or run a gondola end promotion as a means of reaching a large number of relevant consumers with an appropriate message or offer. For many brand owners, the answer is to focus promotional resources in-store, thereby communicating directly with consumers at the point of purchase as opposed to communicating with them through another medium that is not so closely tied to the point of purchase.

The convergence of media and channel choice is the result of the coming together of two trends: progress in brand thinking and the inexorable march of developments in IT. As outlined in Chapter 7, a brand used to be thought of as a lifeless, manipulable entity that was built through advertising. Today, it is seen as a dynamic asset that lives in the consumer's mind: an experience of the value proposition that is created through multiple touchpoints where the organization, wittingly or unwittingly, engages the consumer.

As media choices have expanded and become more sophisticated, opportunities for dialogue with the consumer have grown in a stepwise fashion. Supplying organizations and consumers are no longer restricted to communicating with each other by telephone, facsimile or post, or through face-to-face encounters with in-store staff or sales representatives. New technologies have given rise to personal and interactive media, such as email, the Internet, personal digital assistants (PDAs), mobile phones and the next-generation smart phone. In the process of enriching communication, these developments have expanded the role of IT. IT is now not only concerned with the exchange of information but also with interaction, and with the promise of integration in the near future. Where dialogue can take place, so the option to transact also arises, and the use of media and channels become interwoven.

New Consumer Marketing demands an approach to media and channels that builds on the benefits of media and channel integration. First among these benefits is the ability to develop organizational agility and thus enhance consumer responsiveness. The new range of media and channel choices available offers organizations the opportunity to lower costs, provide better service and personalize the value proposition. The collection and analysis of previously unimaginable kinds of data through increasingly sophisticated technologies makes this possible.

Making the Most of Media Choices

The proliferation of media choices is causing tectonic shifts in marketing thinking about how they can be used to build brands. Media decisions in the production-driven era were about how to advertise to consumers, which was a largely one-way exercise motivated by the desire to control consumer response. In a subsequent phase, more interactive media choices, such as direct response media (e.g. direct mail offers and direct response telephone lines), were used to encourage more continuous communication between consumers and the organization. In the consumption-led economy the aim is connectivity, or the development of a shared understanding that comes from ongoing dialogues, experiences and shared values that develop between a marketer and consumers (Schultz and Lindberg-Repo, 2002). The challenge for marketers today is selecting the most effective and efficient combination of media from the wealth of interactive and non-interactive media options. The goal is to ensure that consumers have a perfect experience across whatever media they use to interact with the organization.

Connectivity enables brand owners to build deeper and more enduring relationships with New Consumers. These relationships are developed through the empowered engagement of both participants in a two-way interaction process, one that is exemplified by Nokia.

Nokia

The Nokia Game is a multimedia, adventure-cum-espionage, role-playing game, which Nokia has been running for the last four years in 18 countries, attracting over half a million players in 2001. Clues are given out to players in a range of ways, including text messaging, voicemail, email, the Internet (see Figure 8.2), TV, radio and the press. The game is based on the 'future of communication', and it educates players on future technologies and applications. Players have to find out about everything from different ringtones and menu systems through to GSM and GPRS in order to progress from one stage of the game to the next.

More than just a form of play, the Nokia Game is a marketing platform that creates Nokia brand advocates by being particularly relevant and credible to a specifically defined audience. The game gets consumers highly involved in the brand by engaging and rewarding them for their attention and thereby creating a virtual Nokia community. In effect, players give Nokia permission to market the company's products to them. In this way the various levels of dialogue – texting, voicemail, press, for example – enable a mutual understanding and reciprocal generation of the value proposition. Players

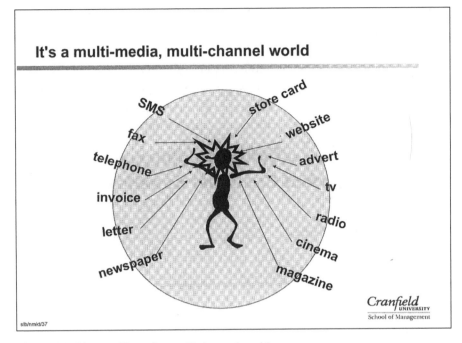

Figure 8.2 It's a multi-media, multi-channel world

gain knowledge and excitement from the game, while Nokia benefits from building knowledge of its consumers. The game grows as the network of players grows, and the bonds between Nokia and the players develop.

'Gaining permission' is a facet of media strategy that has emerged with the coming of the consumption-led economy. New Consumers' highly fragmented lifestyles and time pressures mean that they have less time to meet all the demands on them. They are not the passive subjects of marketers, but discerning and demanding customers. Part of the value exchange in the consumption-led economy relates to the value these consumers get out of investing their attention. As Herbert Simon, Nobel Prize winning economist, has noted, 'Information consumes attention … a wealth of information creates a poverty of attention … the only factor that becomes scarce in a world of abundance is human attention'. Permission marketing (Godin, 1999) has, therefore, developed out of the problems associated with gaining the attention of consumers. Where a marketer receives the consumer's permission, the conscious effort required by the consumer to pay attention more often than not results in dialogue between the two parties.

The challenge for brand owners in making the most of media choices has an external and an internal component. Externally, they are aiming to replicate the experience of a one-to-one relationship where the consumer feels they are being spoken to by the same person in every encounter. The internal challenge is to generate data across the various media to create a single, unified view of the consumer. This single view ensures that, regardless of the medium or channel through which the consumer interacts with the organization, the consumer is recognized and the history of their relationship is remembered. Achieving this single view demands clear objectives in the management of data, issues that are explored later in Chapter 9.

From a consumer perspective, a perfect experience that replicates the feeling of being spoken to by the same person in every brand encounter is most likely to be delivered through a media-neutral strategy. The integrated brand communications strategies adopted by Volkswagen and Stella Artois provide good examples. Volkswagen's multimedia/multi-agency approach has helped the brand double its new car sales and value share within six years. The strategy, which includes the use of PR, direct marketing, online marketing, cinema and radio, led directly to 151,000 extra sales and £1.99 billion extra revenue for VW UK.

Stella Artois

Stella Artois' communications strategy cleverly exploits knowledge of consumer lifestyles and the popular medium of film. Research into the brand's largely young male (aged 18–34) consumer base had revealed that a high majority visited the cinema or rented videos on a regular basis. At a time when most other lager beers were using sport to communicate their brand values, Stella adopted the theme of film. Its communications strategy included: advertisements that possessed a cinematic feel, film sponsorship on Channel 4, film events around the UK, and on-pack promotions for Blockbuster videos. The task of making this theme work across a number of agencies fell to the marketing manager, who appointed a lead agency for each cycle of the strategy. The specialist agencies – in advertising, sales promotions, media buying, consumer and trade public relations, for example – then activated the element of the strategy within their particular medium. Crucial to this way of working is that everyone buys into the same definition of the brand, echoing the need for brand clarity discussed in Chapter 7.

As well as integrating media choices across channels, some brand owners are pioneering integration across a number of brand owners to deliver a perfect experience for consumers. The aim of these brand owners is to cross-promote their own operations and develop long-term marketing partnerships. Disney is one company that has pursued such an integrative approach.

Disney

Disney has a number of cross-media deals with global partners such as Home Depot and McDonald's. In 2001 the DIY chain Home Depot signed a three-year tie-up across Disney's ABC network, ESPN sports channel and Lifetime channel. The deal was reported to be worth £65 million to Disney. As part of the agreement, Disney is launching a range of branded children's paints in Home Depot and has also agreed to purchase Home Depot products for its own operations. Disney's ten-year deal with McDonald's successfully cross-promotes Disney films through children's Happy Meal promotions in McDonald's restaurants.

Making the Most of Channel Choices

In the same way that the proliferation of media choices is causing a shift in thinking about how best to communicate the value proposition, the expansion of marketing channels is challenging thinking about how best to transact value. The brand owner must devise a channel strategy that is appealing to its target consumers and profitable to its business. This may involve the use of a single channel or a combination of channels. The brand owner must choose from an ever-widening range of direct channels (e.g. Internet, telephone, facsimile) and indirect channels (e.g. retailers, distributors and service providers).

As with media strategies, the goal of channel strategies is to ensure that the consumer has a perfect experience across all the channels used. One of the biggest issues for organizations here is to minimize channel conflict. Interactive channels offer organizations the opportunity to transact directly with consumers faster and at a lower cost than most non-interactive channels do. Consequently, many organizations have decided to cut out the middlemen and have ceased using traditional intermediaries. For example, call centre technology allows insurance companies such as Direct Line to offer and transact the value proposition by dealing with consumers directly over the telephone. This obviates the need for expensive networks of insurance brokers and keeps the premiums low, creating mutual benefit for both seller and buyer.

While a strategy of 'disintermediation' may appear seductive at first sight, channel strategy development should be based upon the optimum combination of channels necessary to provide the most effective and efficient means of delivering the value proposition. Different channels offer different advantages (see Figure 8.3). Norwich Union, for example, sells financial products directly to consumers through independent financial advisers (IFAs). The *Guardian* newspaper produces and sells newspapers through intermediaries and also offers an online news service free of charge. Thornton's, the confectioner, transacts its value proposition through a network of shops, by phone, fax and post, and via the Internet.

It is crucial for organizations to understand why their consumers prefer to use one channel rather than another: why, for example, some favour remote interaction while others prefer transacting face-to-face. Identifying and satisfying the channel preferences of New Consumers is particularly challenging, as these may change according to the type of purchase or the time at which the transaction takes place. For instance, consumers may be content to book a weekend trip to Europe using the online facility of a discount airline but may prefer completing the transaction for a lengthier summer trip abroad in a face-to-face encounter. Above all, New Consumers are looking for organizational agility – a supplier who can adapt to their differing needs on different purchasing occasions. Channel strategy decisions therefore need to be reviewed regularly and adjusted as appropriate.

Another popular channel strategy in the consumption-led economy is reintermediation, or the introduction of new types of intermediary. Examples of this include the use of web-enabled information agents, also known as 'infomediaries', who carry out information searches on behalf of prospective purchasers. Some infomediaries not only research products and services on behalf of consumers, but also manage sales transactions and post-sales service agreements. Autobytel, for example, provides information about car prices and purchase availability, and will even facilitate the sale and organize delivery. This one-stop-shop approach is attractive to many New Consumers, who have little time to shop around for best value. Some even engage 'personal shoppers', such as TenUK, to act as their own purchasing agents across a number of sectors.

Organizations such as Conciera, which offers clients a technology platform on which to transform their businesses in line with this buyer-centric

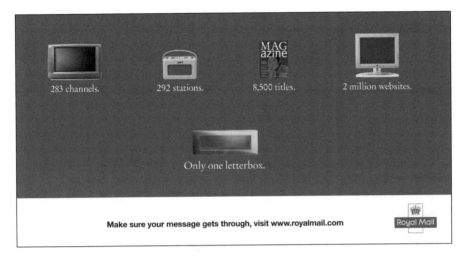

Figure 8.3 This Royal Mail advertisement shows the extent of channel choice
Reproduced by permission of Royal Mail

philosophy, believe that this is where the future of channel strategy development lies – that by acting as the consumer's partner and providing access to a new set of information tools across new media and telephone channels, agent-based businesses will create and deliver new forms of superior customer service and consumer value.

THE ROLE OF SERVICE IN VALUE DELIVERY

The arrival of the consumption-led economy has elevated the role of service in the creation and delivery of the value proposition. Increasingly, organizations are recognizing service as a source of competitive differentiation. Service excellence is seen as a key profitability driver. Southwest Airlines (SWA) and First Direct are examples of organizations that have used service to enhance the consumer's experience of the value proposition. SWA has transformed cabin service into a form of entertainment that is regularly promoted by word-of-mouth recommendation. Similarly, First Direct now offers a remote banking service that consumers have warmed to and are keen to advocate. In both these cases the consumer's experience of the brand is delivered through the actions and attitudes of staff. In effect, the service delivered by staff *is* the brand.

Despite wide acknowledgement of the value of providing high levels of service, many customer-care activities fail to meet buyer and supplier expectations. New Consumers are more demanding and sophisticated in their expectations of service and organizations need to be able to respond accordingly. This requires an ethos of consumer responsiveness within the business, and New Consumer Marketing proposes a living demand system to enable this to flourish. The NCM model acknowledges the importance of employees' contribution to value creation and delivery; this was explored in Chapter 7 and is emphasized further in Chapter 9.

Creating a Service Strategy

To optimize the role of service in the delivery process, it is useful to break service down into its three component stages: pre-transaction, transaction and post-transaction. The pre-transaction elements of service relate to corporate policies or programmes involving written statements of service policy and the planning of strategies for dealing with different types of consumers at various points in their relationship with the organization. The transaction elements comprise the customer service variables that are directly involved in the delivery of the value proposition, such as product availability, order cycle times, service ambience, and so on. Post-transaction elements have to do with the support consumers receive once they take ownership of the product or service. These may include warranties, parts and repair services, complaint procedures, loyalty clubs, and so on.

To ensure a consistent approach across these three stages of the service encounter, exemplary organizations create a service strategy. As suggested by Professor Martin Christopher in his book *The Customer Service Planner* (1992), service strategy involves the identification of a service mission in which the organization articulates its service pledge and the setting of service objectives. These objectives should link back to the insight generated by the organization into the nature of the value consumers are seeking and the consequent analysis of opportunities available. They will thus serve to highlight the importance of service quality variables such as reliability, responsiveness, assurance and empathy. Service strategy can then be refined for different consumer segments, as different clusters of consumers will be looking for different service packages. Once a service package has been developed for each segment, service programmes can be implemented. The Ritz-Carlton Hotel Company is extremely focused on creating exactly the right service levels for its customers.

The Ritz-Carlton Hotel

The Ritz-Carlton Hotel Company has created a value-centric service strategy that is implemented across the world by its 22,000 employees. The company was awarded the Malcolm Baldridge National Quality Award, in 1992 and 1999, and is one of only two companies to have received the award twice. This is a considerable achievement given that the company operates in an industry where high staff turnover rates are the norm. The company's strategy is characterized by an emphasis on generating employee satisfaction based on a belief that this results in customer satisfaction, which in turn delivers greater profitability. The strategy is pursued in a number of ways. For example, each day every member of staff has a meeting with their supervisor, manager, the vice-president or the chief executive at the start of their shift. Although the meeting lasts only 15 minutes, it covers all the essential items, from which VIPs are staying in the hotel to staff suggestions about service improvements. What sets this pre-shift briefing apart from the way other hotel chains organize is that every employee of the company across the world discusses the same subject on the same day. Each day the briefings focus on one of 20 basic service principles, standards that were laid down when the company was formed. The following are a few examples:

No. 10 – Each employee is empowered. For example, when a guest has a problem or needs something special, you should break away from your regular duties to address and resolve the issue.

No. 11 – Uncompromising levels of cleanliness are the responsibility of every employee.

No. 12 – To provide the finest personal service for our guests, each employee is responsible for identifying and recording individual guest preferences.

Source: Tony Mosely, 'Are you being served? The route to good customer care', *Consumer Policy Review*, Nov./Dec., 2002.

Which? Published by Consumers' Association, 2 Marylebone Road, London NW1 4DF, for further information please call 0800 252 100

Recruiting and Motivating Staff

Acknowledgement of the importance of people in delivering service has led to a greater interest in the recruitment, motivation and retention of staff. Research shows that when employees identify with the norms and values of an organization that reflect a commitment to customer service, they are less inclined to leave their jobs. This reduction in employee turnover serves to strengthen the organization. It promotes a culture where service values become embedded in the way things are done and are more easily transmitted to successive generations of employees. Recruitment is, therefore, of crucial importance to organizations. In order to attract and retain the highest quality recruits – those who share the organization's values and will make a major contribution to its future success – organizations have to market themselves to potential recruits as employers of choice. With changing demographics threatening the supply of young people in the West, the so-called 'war for talent' (Michaels et al., 2001) is an everyday reality for many companies.

At the Ritz-Carlton, recruitment is carried out using a number of techniques. Psychometric tests are used to identify candidates with the right work attitude and, by matching their test scores against those of the best performing staff, the company is able to allocate jobs according to individual suitability. New employees undergo a minimum of five interviews but provisional job offers are normally issued within 48 hours of the first interview so that good people are not lost to the competition.

The Ritz-Carlton's approach provides a rich contrast with the way Pret A Manger recruits its staff. Following application and interview, Pret A Manger's prospective candidates are paid to work for one day in one of the company's stores. Staff already working in that store then make the final decision as to whether the candidate is employed. This has the effect of

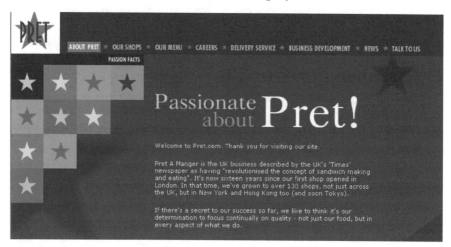

Figure 8.4 Pret A Manger
Reproduced by permission of Pret A Manger

empowering staff and ensuring only people with the 'Pret attitude' (see Figure 8.4), who are able to demonstrate they would uphold Pret A Manger's values and ethos, are taken on. In fact, only about 20% of candidates pass this exacting test.

Staff motivation is another important part of retaining employees. Most organizations use employment benefits and training and development to reward and motivate their employees. As Singapore Airlines demonstrates, these need to fit with the values and culture of the organization and be tailored to improving the overall value-centric ethos and practice of the organization.

Singapore Airlines

Singapore Airlines employs about 8% of Singapore's working population and is consistently voted one of the top local employers. The training of employees is comprehensive – the programme for new stewardesses has been referred to as a 'debutante boot camp', involving four months of social as well as operational skills training. Career development opportunities are strong and staff are regularly appraised as a means of improving their performance. In an effort to retain trained staff who have taken maternity leave, the company operates a 'Flying Mom' scheme, which enables stewardesses with long service records to spend more time at home with their families.

Other successful organizations have evolved similarly unique approaches to motivating staff, which often depend on cross-functional collaboration between marketing, operations and human resources management. It is important that there is alignment between the value proposition offered to consumers and that offered to employees. For example, Countrywide Porter Novelli (CPN) is a successful business-to-business PR consultancy that operates what it calls the 4Is culture:

- Imagination – making our work memorable.
- Irreverence – challenging the status quo.
- Improvement – a little better every time.
- Initiative – making the first move.

This articulation of principles does not simply take the form of a bright logo to be used in communications, but provides a framework for managing delivery of the value proposition both internally and externally. It represents the distinctive advantage CPN believes it offers clients, and guides the recruitment, training and promotion of staff internally. Unusually, the director of personnel and development and the marketing director sit down together and discuss joint implementation of the internal and external marketing strategy on a regular basis.

Empowering Employees to Live the Brand

A New Consumer Marketing approach to service requires the highest levels of consumer responsiveness, and service providers have a great opportunity to make this a differentiated part of the value proposition. What New Consumers are looking for is an individual response to their particular requirements, and those on the so-called front-line of a business are in a position to customize the experience for them. The way employees feel about their job often defines the way they view the brand and the way they communicate it to consumers. For this reason, many organizations see the empowerment of employees as a business priority.

The secret of success here is not so much a mechanistic prescription or a series of instructions to staff, but rather a dialogue where organizations help staff understand what the brand stands for and seeks to accomplish, and what their individual role is in achieving the brand objectives. It is important that employees receive information about organizational performance and that they are rewarded for contributing to it. While 'living the brand' is a common corporate goal, few organizations actually achieve it. A MORI survey carried out in 2002 reported that 30% of UK employees are brand neutral or are not interested in their company's brand, while a further 22% are brand saboteurs, actively working against the brand culture. This means less than half of the country's employees can be considered as brand champions who will spread their companies' brand values. Of these, 33% would talk positively about the brand if asked, and only 15% would talk positively about the brand spontaneously.

Formal communication programmes that aim to market the brand internally are used by many organizations to endow staff with an enhanced potential for yielding profit. For example, Land Rover launched the latest Range Rover with a series of coordinated events for employees, dealers and the press. Part of the strategy was the placement of the car in the *Tomb Raider* movie. Around 20,000 employees at Land Rover were invited to private screenings of the film and encouraged to bring their families, creating great word-of-mouth marketing. British Airways, when faced with orchestrating 50,000 articulations of the brand through its 50,000 staff worldwide, launched the 'Passion for Service' initiative. It is essentially a training session to teach staff about brands, and the BA brand in particular. Having spent £1 million developing Club World and £200 million implementing it, the internal marketing programme is a way of protecting and enhancing that investment. Brand clarity, as discussed earlier in Chapter 7, is a necessary precondition of making staff empowerment work.

Staff empowerment requires trust and courage on the part of the organization as employees are given autonomy to interpret the brand in a way that is both meaningful to them and their job, and to consumers. Tesco, for example, empowers staff to respond to legitimate customer complaints by giving them the authority to replace products or issue reimbursements without having to refer to supervisors. In doing so, the company demonstrates a respect for their employees' ability to assess situations and manage customers. In a similar move, Abbey National has given its front-line staff the power to take decisions such as reimbursing customers who feel they have been charged unfairly. In both these cases, by not passing problem resolution up the chain of command, consumers are made to feel valued and respected. The issue is dealt with quickly, saving expensive company time and ensuring customer satisfaction.

Speed of response in resolving consumer problems is all-important as New Consumers are becoming more marketing literate and less easy to please. Those whose issues are not dealt with swiftly and satisfactorily have the confidence and wherewithal to make their views known across a range of media (as described in Chapter 2). Studies have shown that while up to 98% of dissatisfied customers never complain when they receive poor service, 90% will not return to the disappointing vendor in future as a result of the poor service. Furthermore, consumers who are dissatisfied are likely to tell at least ten others about their poor service experience, whereas a good service experience will be related to only three others. This makes it doubly hard for organizations to gain a reputation for good service and all the more reason for an organization to work hard to maintain a good reputation.

The processes within an organization that are concerned with creating, developing and maintaining an internal service culture and an orientation that enables the organization to achieve its service goals are usually managed as part of an internal marketing strategy. The fundamental aim is to develop awareness of the value proposition sought by both internal and external customers, and to remove functional barriers to organizational performance. The organization must ensure that every employee, whether they are directly or indirectly, frequently or infrequently in contact with external customers, contributes to the delivery of a superior value proposition. Despite the fact that for many organizations internal marketing programmes are a formal part of the way value is transacted, there is no consensus on how these programmes should best be implemented. This is because the importance of internal marketing has only recently been acknowledged and because of the debate that has arisen about exactly who within an organization should have responsibility for it. This topic is returned to in Chapter 9.

THE ROLE OF TECHNOLOGY INTEGRATION IN VALUE DELIVERY

The integration of technology into service delivery is transforming many businesses, and Petcareco Limited is a useful example of this. Petcareco is a one-stop pet resort and care centre based in Washington, Tyne and Wear, which looks after pets (mainly cats and dogs) while their owners are on holiday (see Figure 8.5). As part of the service, all sorts of creature comforts – from TVs to sofas – can be added to a pet's temporary 'apartment'. A hydrotherapy pool and a bespoke vet service complement the pet care services. The business is staffed by a team of dedicated animal lovers who are supported in their work by a sophisticated, but easily manageable, range of technology. For example, handheld devices are used to carry daily pet care schedules and a back office system records data on every pet, enabling the company to instantly recognize and recall any previous 'guest' history, and use it to make the pet feel welcome and at home. The aim is to ensure that every animal gets the right service, at the right time, in the right place.

The aim of integrating technology into service delivery is to optimize the use of available media and channels. Again, the goal is to ensure that the consumer has a perfect experience across all media and channels used. Integration in today's complex and demanding marketing environment requires moving away from the conventional approach to media and

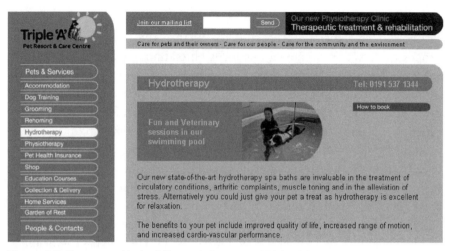

Figure 8.5 Petcareco Limited (formerly known as Triple 'A')
Reproduced by permission of Triple A Animal Hotel & Care Centre

channel strategy, which has been to have different specialist agencies manage various elements of the marketing mix, while consumer enquiries are dealt with at an external call centre.

When call centres first appeared in the UK they were held up as the future of customer service. By offering a central point of customer contact, the call centre was seen as the answer to a comprehensive approach to customer service. It is estimated that there are currently around 6,000 call centres in Britain and the number is expected to rise to 8,000 by 2005. The UK call centre industry now employs almost 500,000 people, or 1.7% of the working population. However laudable and popular an idea, the call centre's reputation has tarnished over time due to adverse publicity and dreadful consumer experiences. In too many cases these centres have been exposed as a means of cutting costs rather than improving service levels. Some organizations, however, go to great lengths to make their call centres as 'human' and customer-friendly as possible. Virgin Mobile's call centre is located at its headquarters in Wiltshire. The centre is light, airy and divided into sections staffed by different teams that work in light-hearted competition with each other. Egg's communications centre in Derby has also employed new concepts in lighting, colour and space. Its teams work in mini-communities and comfy chillout zones create a positive working environment. A pleasant working environment helps keep staff motivation high, and this in turn has a positive impact on customer satisfaction.

The unique feature of these two companies' call centres is that they use technology as a means to an end: to enhance the delivery of the value proposition. When organizations focus on technology as an end in itself, value-centricity is unattainable. The challenge is deciding where and how to integrate technology into the implementation of service strategy. The decision-making process is made easier where the organization has a service blueprint, or map of its service processes.[2] This effectively reduces service encounters – or all points of contact between the consumer and the organization – to a series of interrelated steps and sequences, as the example in Figure 8.6 shows. It offers an opportunity to review service strengths and weaknesses and plan resource allocation more appropriately as well as to communicate responsibilities throughout the organization.

Multichannel centres are now emerging as the next generation of contact centre. Call centres are becoming web enabled, and consumers can make contact with the organization according to their channel preference. In some cases in the US, for example, call-centre staff are being replaced by technology that plugs into the software that runs the company's website. Virtual call-centre operators, or V-Rep's, who can talk to, and understand, customers, are taking their places. The range of options now available to an organization affords a high level of flexibility, as the case of Nestlé demonstrates.

Nestlé

Nestlé is testing this new approach to multichannel customer management. The company is seeking to manage and execute everything – from the creation of one-to-one consumer communications through to generating and responding to phone, fax, post and email enquiries – from a dedicated communications centre. The project has been piloted in France at a 'relationship centre' set up by McCann Relationship Marketing Paris (MRM), a division of McCann Erickson World Group, Nestlé's advertising agency.

Nestlé has promoted details about how to contact the company on products since the 1960s. However, in 2000 this became a more forceful invitation for French consumers to make contact when Nestlé introduced its Nestlé en Direct scheme. This initiative, along with Club Nestlé, a club for consumers, forms the basis of Nestlé's consumer relationship activity in France. Both activities are used to encourage consumers to communicate with the company and provide their personal details. Nestlé uses this data to segment consumers and to tailor one-to-one promotional and marketing activity.

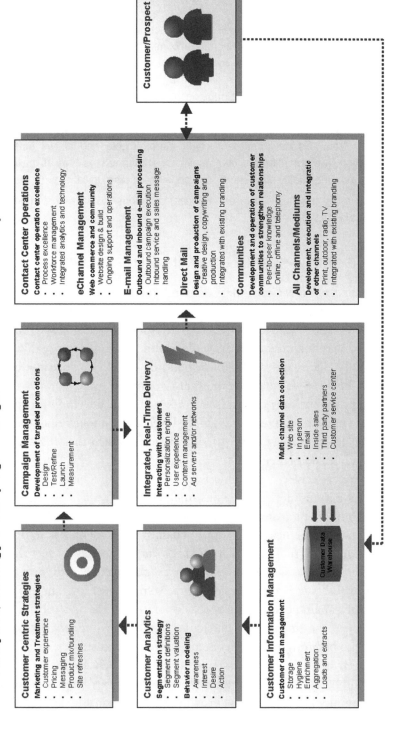

Figure 8.6 Customer contact, communications and relationship process. *Source:* Dr Raymond Pettit, New Jersey Institute of Technology

To manage all these activities more effectively, Nestlé has taken the innovative step of creating a multichannel communications centre under one roof. All forms of enquiry made by French consumers to the company – an estimated 200,000 a year – are handled by MRM's relationship centre. In moving response handlers alongside advertising creatives, customer intelligence experts, new media, branding and management consultants, the consumer is put at the heart of the business. Nestlé foresees a number of benefits from this new approach. It is more flexible and allows better integration between different communications channels as well as giving control over the quality of all one-to-one consumer communications.

Source: Meg Carter, 'Towards a closer relationship with customers', *Financial Times*, 11 March 2002.

THE ROLE OF THE SUPPLY CHAIN IN VALUE DELIVERY

As we have seen, New Consumers demand goods and services through an ever-changing mix of media and channels. Meeting their requirements for faster, better and cheaper service and delivery depends heavily on the make-up and robustness of the supply chain. Only those organizations whose supply chains are capable of responding rapidly to volatile demand will thrive in this post-quake business environment.

Increasingly, business theorists are talking about developing demand-led supply chains to deliver the required level of consumer responsiveness. This means moving away from the simplistic approach that characterized supply-chain management in the production-driven era. Then, supply chains were relatively unsophisticated: extending forwards through distributors and retailers to the consumer and then stretching backwards through component assemblers to the suppliers of the raw materials. Supply chains were linear, and supply-chain management was to do with managing delivery trucks and storage sheds (or so it seemed). Over the past two decades supply chains have grown in complexity, and many now resemble 'webs' or 'networks' of collaborative relationships. The evolution of the supply-chain network has been accelerated by the application of IT. The impact of the Internet, in particular, has enabled widely distributed operations to be brought together at a relatively low cost.

This network, or 'extended enterprise', approach to managing the supply chain has developed in response to the downward pressures on price arising from global overcapacity, growing competition and more powerful customers (issues that were discussed in Chapter 3). Falling market prices compel organizations to turn their focus inwards and to concentrate on reducing costs. Over the past decade, rationalization within the supply chain has been a major source of cost savings. The idea of 'lean manufacturing', promulgated by James Womack[3] at MIT in the early 1990s, has attracted considerable interest. Based on the production system used in Japanese-owned automobile manufacturing plants, particularly that of Toyota, the idea was later extended to form the wider concept of the 'lean enterprise'. The focus of this approach is the elimination of waste and the creation of competitive advantage through lower cost prices. Critics argue that it only works well where demand is relatively stable and hence predictable, and where the requirement for variety is low. In today's more volatile markets, where consumer requirements stipulate more product variety and where the ability to forecast demand is diminishing, a different approach is called for.

Competing through the Supply Chain

As pointed out by Professor Martin Christopher of Cranfield School of Management, nowadays it is supply chains rather than companies that compete in the marketplace (Christopher and Peck, 1997; Christopher, 1998). One of the clearest examples of an organization that competes through its supply chain is Dell.

Dell

Michael Dell eschewed the use of conventional channels to distribute his PCs and focused instead on direct sales. Consumers can select their own PC configuration online at Dell.com, and within just 90 minutes, their personally customized 'grey box' will roll off the factory's production line. Dell's suppliers have built their factories close by and inventory is down to four days, making Dell the number one computer service provider in the world. When Dell did attempt to break into established retail distribution channels in the early 1990s, it all went badly wrong and the company pulled out after suffering its first ever loss. The direct sales model offers Dell a structural advantage that rivals IBM and Hewlett-Packard do not have.

Source: Amanda Hall, 'The boy who lived the American dream', *The Sunday Times*, 1 December 2002; Michael Dell and Catherine Fredman (1999); Michael Dell (2002).

Acceptance of the philosophy that it is supply chains that compete with one another, rather than companies, has led organizations to acknowledge their strengths and weaknesses and to outsource those activities they believe can be performed more cost-effectively by others. The supply chain has, in effect, become a confederation of closely linked specialists whose cooperative behaviour creates a highly differentiated value chain.

Often it is not technology that is the barrier to making these complex partnerships work, but lack of trust. As highlighted in Chapter 3, the sharing of information and expertise previously considered confidential is essential in building the degree of trust necessary for collaboration. A number of major retailers have already begun the process of implementing this collaborative approach to strategy making, setting up private web-based exchanges requiring the integration of both parties' internal systems to share data and ideas. Building these closer relationships between businesses can be very beneficial. Some estimate that the introduction of e-procurement systems founded on joint working arrangements can shorten order fulfilment cycles by 70% and cut administration costs by 50–70%. It is even believed that inventory costs can be halved – a significant benefit considering that holding stocks of unsold goods is a primary cost escalator.

Consumer Responsiveness through Time Compression

Consumer responsiveness is dependent on superior levels of insight, innovation and agility. As far as the supply chain goes, the focus has to be on the elimination of time, rather than of waste. The aim of time compression in supply chains is to shorten the total pipeline time between the procurement of materials and payment for the finished goods. In most organizations it takes longer to procure, make and deliver the finished product to the customer than the customer is prepared to wait, giving rise to a mismatch in expectations that is known to as the 'lead-time gap'. Normally organizations overcome this problem by carrying 'buffer' or surplus stock. The amount of inventory is typically based on a forecast of what the market will require. However, forecasting is a far from accurate science. As Martin Christopher says, organizations that manage to close this lead-time gap 'need neither forecasts nor inventory, making them more responsive to customer demand and able to reduce the cost of financing the pipeline' (Christopher, 2001).

Establishing partnerships with other members of the supply chain is one of the most critical ways in which organizations can develop a more responsive supply chain. This usually involves a rationalization of the supplier base, as it is easier to develop closer relationships with a smaller number of strategic suppliers rather than trying to manage closer relationships with hundreds or thousands of suppliers. These relationships are characterized by synchronized operations and the transparency of information. The Zip Project at Marks & Spencer is an example of this new way of working.

Zip

Zip is a joint venture between Marks & Spencer and Desmond, a long-standing supplier to Marks & Spencer based in Northern Ireland, that was created as part of a wider plan to enable Marks & Spencer to escape its well-publicized woes of the late 1990s. The company had to face up to the fact that it was not delivering fashion fast enough to the shop floor and its prices were not competitive. Zip is designed to provide Marks & Spencer with greater competitive advantage in the area of children's clothing through improved supply-chain management. Marks & Spencer has made cost savings by changing its traditional relationships with suppliers, eliminating areas of duplication and increasing the speed with which its goods come to market. Traditionally, suppliers created the goods and brought them to the buying teams at Marks & Spencer, who then decided which goods had the greatest appeal. Marks & Spencer has now brought much of this design function in-house.

Under the new arrangements, Zip's London office is responsible for the design work and fabric development while samples are developed in Northern Ireland. Samples are costed and different suppliers, including Desmond itself, then bid to produce the finished garment. The advantage of this approach is that Zip retains the copyright on the designs, and their manufacture can therefore be shifted from supplier to supplier as required or as capacity becomes available – Marks & Spencer uses 120 different suppliers in 28 countries. Having greater consistency and control over production realizes savings that can be passed on to consumers. The biggest advantage, however, lies in the reduced amount of time it takes to get a design on to the shop floor: the organization can react quickly to the fickleness of pre-teen fashion. Traditionally, this process has taken 28 weeks; Zip aims to reduce this to 12 weeks. The potential rewards are great as children's wear accounts for about 10% of Marks & Spencer's non-food sales, worth between £300 and £400 million.

Source: Martin Waller, 'M&S takes a fresh route to childhood', *The Times*, 7 September 2002.

Another way of closing the lead-time gap is through rationalizing internal processes. The key here is to remove all non-value-adding processes. 'Value-adding time' activities create a benefit for which consumers are prepared to pay. 'Non-value-adding time' activities do not create customer benefit and are a drain on company resources. One of the most effective means of creating a value-adding culture within the organization is to focus externally on the value proposition that consumers are seeking. Guinness achieved this in the mid-1990s by basing an overhaul of its business processes on insight generated into what consumers wanted from the company.

Guinness

In the mid-1990s, Guinness was one of the few large brewers not to own any licensed premises (pubs and clubs) in the UK. The company relied on consumer demand to persuade its trade customers (those who owned the routes to market, largely other brewery companies) to stock its products. Guinness stout held sales remarkably well in a declining market for dark coloured beers but in the early 1990s competition was heightened by the launch of rival stouts, such as Murphy's, and the rising popularity of imported bottled beers. Faced with the threat of more vigorous competition, Guinness undertook a review of its business and, as a consequence, set about improving its performance in the marketplace.

Guinness invested heavily in a brewery upgrade to ensure the quality of its product but was dissatisfied with the results of its insight generation activity, which revealed that consumers were often disappointed with the quality of a

Figure 8.7 Guinness' 'Perfect Pint'

pint of Guinness consumed in different outlets. Guinness, like other cask beers, is a 'live' product and needs to be stored and handled carefully. Where procedures are not followed, the result is an experience of variable quality for consumers. What consumers were looking for was expressed as 'the perfect pint in every pub'.

Guinness used this insight to inform internal decision making about which processes needed to be in place to ensure consistent delivery of the perfect pint, enabling them to create a cross-functional approach to business. Guinness worked with its partners in the supply chain to educate the pub trade about the importance of looking after the product and serving it correctly. This was a three-stage operation, known as 'the pour, the settle, the top up', and it provided a focus for training in-house staff in pubs and clubs (see Figure 8.7). Consumers were also targeted with an award-winning advertising campaign that extolled the virtues of waiting for a perfect pint. This coordinated range of activities, based on a clear strategy, propelled Guinness to achieve its highest ever share of the total draught market.

Source: Presentation by Julian Spooner at Cranfield School of Management, January 1996.

A third method of improving consumer responsiveness through supply-chain management is by maximizing the potential of each customer interface. The aim is to be able to capture information on probable demand from consumers as close to the final point of consumption as possible. A real breakthrough in data collection has been achieved by linking buyers' and suppliers' information systems, through initiatives such as Efficient Consumer Response (ECR), Quick Response (QR) and Electronic Data Interchange (EDI). ECR, an attempt to bring about more effective collaboration across all supply-chain members, is most closely associated with the grocery industry, where it is designed to integrate and rationalize product assortment, promotions, new product development and replenishment across the supply chain. QR was developed in the USA to help clothing businesses compete against lower priced imports. By taking a total supply chain view of an industry, QR makes it possible to understand overall performance and the causes of poor performance, and to identify opportunities for improvement. EDI, a technology for broadcasting demand data, was the forerunner of web-enabled systems and is still widely used by larger suppliers.

The advantage of systems integration among supply-chain partners is that it enables the different parties to act on the same aggregate data in a real-time environment. Each partner can gain a clearer picture of consumer demand than they would otherwise be able to obtain independently, and greater consumer responsiveness can be achieved throughout the supply chain. The benefits of such collaboration within knowledge management and operational systems are especially important in developing key accounts,[4] as these normally command a higher strategic value.

The importance of being able to act on real-time demand data becomes more acute the more volatile the market. This is particularly the case with suppliers of fashionable or weather-dependent goods and services, whose competitive survival depends on rapid reactions to unpredictable market changes. For an organization like Britvic, which markets and manufactures its own brands, such as Tango, as well as canning and distributing Pepsi-Cola in the UK, demand for soft drinks can double on hot days. In situations where the product has a limited shelf life or the organization has an obligation to meet high trade-customer service levels, stock-outs cannot be tolerated. Access to instant, accurate and complete demand data is critical to the running of flexible manufacturing operations that aim to ensure constant availability. Indeed, availability becomes a more critical measure of consumer responsiveness than productivity in today's marketplace.

While some suppliers favour a strategy of rapid stock replenishment as a way of managing the amount of inventory they carry, others follow a strategy of postponement, or delaying the finishing or value-adding activities until customer orders have been received. The clothing manufacturer and retailer Zara, for example, purchases a high proportion of its fabric in an undyed (or grey) state. On receipt of incoming orders, the fabric is dyed, patterned and finished by a fully owned subsidiary, which is a supplier to Zara as well as to other manufacturers. By working in this way, Zara is able to originate a design and have the finished goods in its stores within weeks, as opposed to the traditional industry model, which may take up to six months.

Advances in supply-chain thinking are driving the concept more towards the notion of demand-chain management, which is totally in keeping with New Consumer Marketing (Gattorna, 1998). By its very nature, a supply chain focuses on making the flow of product from source to end user as efficient as possible. In contrast, a demand chain focuses on meeting market needs in the most relevant, timely and cost-effective way. In other words, a demand system sees the 'pipeline' as driven from the consumer end, placing the emphasis on consumer responsiveness rather than vendor efficiency. The differences between these two approaches are summarized in Table 8.1.

Table 8.1 Agile supply chain management versus a traditional approach

Agile approach	Traditional approach
Stock is held at the fewest points in the supply chain, if at all, with finished goods sometimes being delivered direct from factory to customer	Stock is held at multiple points in the supply chain, and inventory strategy is often based on organizational and legal ownership considerations
Replenishment of all stocking points is driven from actual sales/usage data collected at the customer interface	Replenishment is driven sequentially by transfers from one stocking point to another
Production is planned across functional boundaries from vendor to customer, through highly integrated systems, with minimum lead times	Production is planned by discrete organizational units with batch feeds between discrete systems
Majority of stock is held as 'work in progress' awaiting build/configuration instructions	Majority of stock is fully finished goods, dispersed geographically, waiting to be sold

Source: Adapted from Christopher (2001)

Agile Supply Chain Management vs a Traditional Approach by Robbins. Prentice Hall 2003. Reprinted by permission of Prentice Hall 3rd ed

This third cell of the New Consumer Marketing model marks the point at which the symbiotic relationship with the consumer is developed. The value that has been defined and created is finally delivered to the marketplace and exchanged with the consumer. While the process of value delivery is contingent on the interplay of media and channels, service, technology integration and the supply chain, it is the role of organizational agility that is of fundamental importance.

SUMMARY POINTS

- Organizational agility is an enterprise-wide concept that demands an ability to change gear and immerse the organization in new opportunities on a continual basis.

- Media choice is to do with how the value proposition is *communicated*, while channel choice is about how it is *transacted*. However, at touchpoints where consumers can be engaged in dialogue, the opportunity for transaction arises, leading to the interrelationship of the two as an integrated media and channel strategy.

- The goal of a multimedia/multi-channel strategy is to ensure that the consumer has a perfect experience across all the media and channels used. Each time the consumer comes into contact with a brand, they should feel like they are talking to the same person.

- Service is an important differentiator in the marketplace. The way in which service staff deal with consumers simultaneously creates and delivers value at the point of consumption. In effect, the value experience *is* the brand.

- The recruitment, motivation and retention of staff are key elements in a successful service strategy.

- Empowering employees takes trust and courage on the part of the organization as employees are given autonomy to interpret the brand in a way that is both meaningful to them and their job, and to consumers.

- Supply chains play a major role in determining consumer responsiveness and competitive advantage. In the new marketplace supply chains must become demand-led.

- Consumer responsiveness requires a supply-chain focus on the elimination of time, rather than of waste. Availability becomes the key measure, rather than productivity.

Demand System Management 9

Seven elements of organizational 'DNA' make a demand system viable.

Managing a demand system is fundamentally different to managing a supply system. It requires turning the supply chain on its head, and taking the consumer as the organization's starting point and not its final destination. As established early on in this book, New Consumers are sophisticated and demanding, and they inhabit an interactive, rather than a static, marketplace. To succeed in this challenging and ever-changing marketing environment, organizations must adopt a value-centric orientation. By focusing on delivering the value consumers actually need and want, organizations can make the radical transition from operating in a production-driven to operating in a consumption-led economy.

The New Consumer Marketing model (see Figure 9.1) draws on learning from the living sciences and conceptualizes the marketing process as three organic cells of a living demand system. Having discussed the nature and function of each of the three cells – value definition, value creation and value delivery – in Chapters 6–8, it is now appropriate to examine how the cells work together, and what organizational elements control and inform their performance.

The way in which these cells collaborate to keep the demand system alive and effective is dependent on the make-up of the 'organizational DNA'. In biology, DNA is the material that carries an organism's genetic information, such as that needed by cells to make enzymes. Enzymes are important because they control the processes that occur within cells. They determine which chemicals are made in a cell and what the cell will do. The information about which enzyme to make and when, has to be permanently stored in each cell so that it can be drawn upon as necessary. The

relationship between biological DNA and enzymes provides a good metaphor for understanding the elements that inform and trigger what happens in a market-driven organization.

Organizational DNA consists of seven elements that fall into two types: those that are people related (intuition, culture and structure, leadership, vision and values, employees) and those that are process related (knowledge management, planning, measurement). Each element carries information to the three cells: value definition, value delivery and value creation. This information enables each cell to optimize performance, thereby ensuring the competitive survival of the organization as a whole. Operating an effective demand system requires an understanding of the role and impact of all of these elements in order that they can be expertly managed. The main challenges facing New Consumer Marketing (to meet the needs of brand owners and retailers, to embrace the New Consumer, to develop real consumer responsiveness, and to arrest the crisis in marketing) reinforce the imperative of addressing these business aspects in a systemic manner.

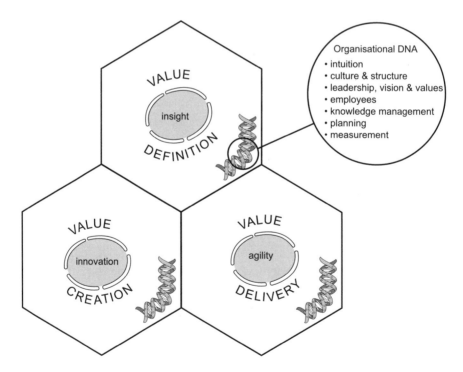

Figure 9.1 The New Consumer Marketing model

New Consumer Marketing breaks out of the binary thinking that has seen businesses swing between a focus on process and a focus on people. Instead, it combines the two by identifying the key processes and relationships that underpin the organization, and using them to help the organization become as adaptable and competitive as possible.

The seven elements of organizational DNA are:

- Intuition
- Culture and structure
- Leadership, vision and values
- Employees
- Knowledge management
- Planning
- Measurement.

THE ROLE OF INTUITION IN DEMAND SYSTEM MANAGEMENT

The mechanistic approach to management, so characteristic of the production-driven era, was based on rational systems that appealed to the reasoning skills of managers. These systems were presented as if there were some underlying algorithm for doing business. Today, management is about engaging both our rational and our creative abilities. Increasing importance is being placed on corporate intuition and imagination. Intuitive ability plays a major role in demand system management by contributing to the development of insight, innovation and organizational agility.

In the definition, creation and delivery of the value proposition, the capacity to instantly understand other people's behaviour, thoughts, wishes, feelings and beliefs is a means of gaining additional perspective. Through intuitive understanding, managers and staff can perceive the truth of things without reasoning or analysis. They can put themselves in the consumer's shoes and see the benefit of taking a particular course of action without needing any rational validation.

Anthropologists believe that this capability is linked to the early social development of humans, particularly with our ability to interact with and influence others. The ability of managers to understand mental states – both their own and those of others – is known as Theory of Mind. Theory of

Mind has been described as 'a start-up kit for learning about the mental world'.[1] It is a kind of 'mind reading', which psychologists refer to as intuitive mentalizing. Encouraging intuitive input in a demand system stimulates innovative thought and a sense of empathy with consumers. This can lead to improvements in the market relevance of the value proposition and thus enhancement of the consumer's experience of the brand.

Most successful entrepreneurs have strong intuitive mentalizing skills, and they use these to put their 'good ideas' about what consumers want into the marketplace. They are able to imagine what the value proposition should look like and to marshal the organization's resources to deliver it. In heavily managed organizations this ability is often repressed. Take, for example, Woburn Safari Park, part of the Woburn estate in Bedford, England, where the importance of intuition is fully recognized.

Woburn Safari Park

At Woburn Safari Park, this elusive 'second sight' has been developed under the leadership of chief executive Chris Webster. Ten years ago the park was in severe decline, but a remarkable turnaround in performance has been achieved through some radical thinking. On the basis of gut feel, the decision was taken to introduce a junior board of 11-year-olds to shadow the park's

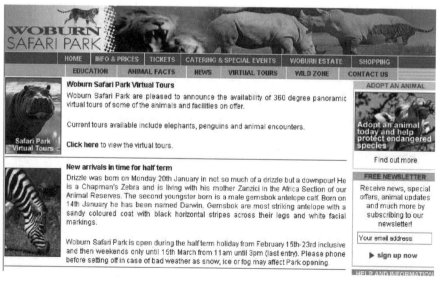

Figure 9.2 Woburn Safari Park
By kind permission of the Marquess of Tavistock

management board. For the family-oriented attraction, engaging the input of young imaginations in strategy making was a wise move: children, of course, do not hold back in asking the why/why not questions. Benchmarking visits are made by the junior board to rival attractions and the children's ideas are assimilated into the way Woburn Safari Park defines, creates and delivers its value proposition.

Intuitive mentalizing is a very necessary ability in the delivery of service. As discussed in Chapter 8, front-line staff need to be able to demonstrate empathy with consumers if they are to convey consumer value in a consistent and personalized way. Where intuitive ability is lacking, the organization will have difficulty in predicting the behaviour of consumers, reading their intentions and understanding their motives and emotions. At worst, the organization will suffer from lack of commitment and motivation to please. The key challenge is to find ways of unleashing the potential for corporate intuition. Intuition is an ability, not a function; it must be embedded within the organization and cannot sit isolated in one department. The development of corporate intuition lies in making it a shared approach to defining, creating and delivering value, and this can best be achieved through the organizational culture and structure.

THE ROLE OF CULTURE AND STRUCTURE IN DEMAND SYSTEM MANAGEMENT

Culture

Organizational culture is one of the most intangible elements of a demand system. Its roots reach deep into the collection of beliefs and assumptions that are commonly held in the organization, and its influence on organizational performance is all pervasive. Organizational culture provides a guide to acceptable internal behaviour, summarized as 'the way things are done around here'. Culture therefore underpins a value-centric business strategy.

Trying to understand organizational culture can be as difficult for those inside the organization as for those outside it. A useful tool for surfacing the behaviours and artefacts that characterize a particular organization is the culture web, developed by academic researchers Professor Gerry Johnson and Kevin Scholes (1992). This is shown in Figure 9.3. The

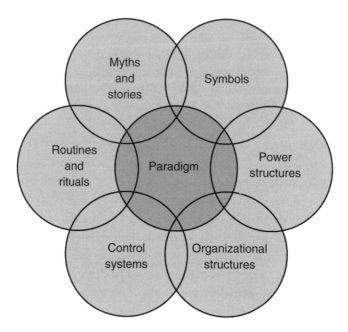

Figure 9.3 The cultural web of an organization. Adapted from Johnson and Scholes (1992)

Exploring Corporate Strategies. Johnson and Scholes, 1998. Reprinted by permission of Pearson Education Limited

culture web makes explicit the rituals of organizational life – the daily routines that are often taken for granted, but which all employees must learn when they join the organization. It captures the stories told about people – the 'heroes' and the 'mavericks' – whose fate symbolizes what the organization is all about. The culture web also notes the symbols that convey meaning within the organization – the use of logos, the allocation of offices and car parking spaces, etc.

Depicting cultural aspects in this way helps in identifying the managerial groups closely associated with the essence of organizational culture, a power structure that may not accord with the official company organigram. The formalized ways in which the organization works – using committees or working parties, for example – also reflect the power structure and send signals throughout the company and its supply chain about what is deemed important. In many organizations there is an incongruity between the values that are promoted and the behaviours that are rewarded. A familiar example is the sales team that is told to maximize customer profitability while being rewarded on the basis of unit sales. The team is tempted to offer discounts and inducements to customers, as the overriding message is 'maximize volume, rather than profits'. Each of these aspects that make up the cultural web can be characterized for an individual organization. As Figure 9.3 shows, at the heart of culture is an underlying paradigm within which the organization operates, made up of the core beliefs, assumptions and values that matter to it.

Closely related to culture is the climate within the organization. This has been summed up by researchers as 'the feeling in the air' that one gets from walking around a company (Clark, 1999). Organizational climate can be created by employees observing what happens to them and what goes on around them, and drawing their own conclusions about the organization's priorities and what it values. Employees then set their own priorities accordingly about where they should focus their energies and competencies, which, in turn, feed back into the organizational climate. Organizational culture and climate are, therefore, dynamic and sensitive to managerial influence. Tesco is an example of an organization that has mastered the management of these intangible aspects and used them to guide the development of a value-centric strategy.

Tesco

In 1992, the issue of organizational culture formed one of the foundation blocks of Tesco's 'First Class Service' initiative, which has since propelled the company to a dominant market position. It represented a shift from the company's previous command-and-control approach to management. Each member of Tesco's then 130,000 staff was empowered to look after customers in the way they thought best. At the same time, managers were encouraged to recognize staff achievements and to set an example by treating them as individuals, so that they would in turn treat customers as individuals. This initiative was highly successful, not least because staff were made aware through internal marketing programmes that the average potential lifetime spend of a Tesco customer was significant, amounting to around £90,000.

Source: 'Tesco Clubcard Forever?', case study, H. Peck, Cranfield School of Management, 2002.

There are, however, pitfalls in encouraging everyone in the company to think in the same way, which can easily happen when everyone is focused on the same goals. The danger is that the organization can fall into the trap of approaching every problem, no matter how different, in the same way. What is required is a management body that supports an innovative culture; one that encourages staff to think and respond differently, but that is nonetheless focused on the organization's vision and informed by its values. A value-centric orientation within the organization ensures these different ways of working are still legitimate. Dell is one organization that manages its organizational culture very effectively.

Dell

Dell's innovative culture supports risk taking and learning from failure. As Michael Dell says, 'to encourage people to innovate more, you have to make it safe for them to fail'. Dell achieves this by creating an internal culture that questions the status quo and encourages smart experimentation. At Dell, failure is seen as a learning experience and is typically considered an important milestone on the road to achieving success. The nature of the business means there is little relevant history for it to draw upon, forcing the organization to create its own response to the challenges it faces. Dell managers also embrace an experimental attitude to decision making. Sometimes it is not possible to wait for the relevant data before making a decision. Under these circumstances, managers are encouraged to make the best possible decisions based on experience, intuition, available data and an assessment of risk.

Source: Amanda Hall, 'The boy who lived the American dream', *The Sunday Times*, 1 December 2002; Michael Dell and Catherine Fredman (1999); Michael Dell (2002).

Tesco and Dell have used organizational culture as the basis of competitive advantage. Organizations that do not heed the importance of managing internal culture effectively can fall prey to strategic drift and become increasingly incapable of self-renewal and self-determination. In effect, organizational culture determines business fate. It is critical to the successful implementation of a demand system that the prevailing culture in the organization supports and drives the development of insight, innovation and agility – the competencies that lie at the heart of each of the three cells of the New Consumer Marketing model.

Structure

The culture of an organization is embodied within the structure of the organization. Traditional vertical organizations, which are hierarchically structured and functionally oriented, work to optimize individual functions at the expense of the entire business and the relationship with the consumer. Hierarchical structures work well when the marketing environment is stable and demand is predictable. Now that the certainties of the production-driven era have been replaced by the uncertainties of the consumption-led economy, flatter, horizontal organizational structures are emerging.

These flatter, horizontal structures enable organizations to be more responsive by speeding up decision-making processes and encouraging cross-functional collaboration, which helps maximize consumer value and operational cost-effectiveness. Value-centric organizations draw key employees together in autonomous, multidisciplinary teams to focus resources around value definition, creation and delivery. Often these teams are temporary, enabling the organization to combine and recombine assets according to the nature of the opportunities that arise. These are firms that regard the organizational whole as greater than the sum of its parts.

However, this does not mean that organizations cannot grow big. Tesco, for example, is one of a small number of organizations that has succeeded in building the virtues of smallness into a large organization, one that now numbers around 200,000 employees. The company achieves this, in part, by having a shared understanding of what the business is aiming for. This draws from the company's clearly stated mission – 'to continually increase value for customers, to earn their lifetime loyalty' – and its corporate values. These values are embedded into the organization through a variety of HR practices that focus on appraisal and reward systems.

The strength of less hierarchically structured organizations lies not just in what they achieve as a single entity but in the power of the network they build around them, through joint ventures, strategic alliances and partnerships. This is the concept of the 'extended enterprise' and its success depends on a new type of logic; one that demands openness and cooperation (with consumers, customers, suppliers and competitors). The extended, or networked, enterprise places greater emphasis on the role of leadership, vision and values.

THE ROLE OF LEADERSHIP, VISION AND VALUES IN DEMAND SYSTEM MANAGEMENT

Leadership

Leadership in organizational management is more important than ever before in this post-quake business environment. Businesses must align their organizational philosophy and practices with the realities of the consumption-led economy. How an organization is led and managed in this time of transition is a key differentiator in the marketplace. While there is no standard formula for what makes an effective leader, New Consumer Marketing demands a number of essential leadership skills.[2]

First among these skills is the ability to engage others in the business's mission. Leaders like Howard Schultz, whose Starbucks business grew profits by 92% to $181.2 million on sales of $3 billion in 2001, have to be able to engage their employees in providing exceptional service to numerous consumers every day. Starbucks, for example, serves 20 million people a week across 5,000 outlets. Key to achieving a dedicated workforce is the ability to communicate the corporate vision effectively to all stakeholders with a distinctive and compelling voice. Internal communications form the most important part of this task and marketers are well placed to manage them, as the essence of the internal communications process is similar to that of the external communications process. It is also important, for strategic reasons, that both processes are aligned, and marketers possess all the relevant skills for managing this.

Secondly, effective leadership provides focus, inspiration and meaning, which need to be communicated to everyone within the organization. The measure of a leader's effectiveness can often be seen in the way he or she manages this communication process. Powerful communicators are good at telling stories, utilizing the potency of metaphors and language. Kjell Nordström and Jonas Ridderstråle, the Swedish economics experts who co-authored the best-selling book, *Funky Business* (2000), suggest that 'communicating a vision not only involves repetition and a carefully distilled message; it demands the ability to tell a story. True leaders are CSOs – Chief Storytelling Officers'.

Senior managers at TGI Friday's restaurants have been telling the same stories for many years, many of them based on the original stories told by founder Dan Skoggins. These work-related stories serve to convey the vision and ethos of the company. The 'employee cloak theory', for example, says: 'You were hired for your personality. When you put on your uniform, don't let it become a cloak and hide yourself behind it. You are not expected to be a robot; in fact we believe our success comes from our interaction with the guests. Work hard, have fun, make money'.

The third essential leadership skill required for New Consumer Marketing to succeed is integrity, including a strong set of personal values. A sense of virtuousness is vital because organizational leaders become the de facto keepers of their company's vision and values. In today's more transparent business environment, they need to be able to inspire commitment among employees. This will not be forthcoming where professional integrity is lacking, as a number of CEOs who have transgressed the boundaries of honourable behaviour have found. Careless remarks made in public that appear to denigrate the company's vision and values may be seized upon by the media, making the task of motivating employees much harder.

Finally, it goes without saying that business leadership demands an ability to grasp the importance of the tectonic shift that has taken place in the marketing environment. This, in turn, implies a steadfast ability to weigh a number of factors and make appropriate decisions to ensure the organization operates effectively and efficiently in defining, creating and delivering the value consumers are seeking.

Vision

All organizations need a shared idea of why they exist and what they are meant to achieve. Vision and values work to support the organization's mission by providing answers to those key questions: 'where are we going?' and 'how are we going to get there?'. Answering them becomes more of an imperative in today's volatile marketplace. This is because vision and values play an important part in realizing a value-centric orientation. They force the organization to think strategically about the long term while providing a framework for coping with turbulence in the short term. With a strong vision and firm values in place, senior managers can delegate responsibilities with more confidence, local managers can get a clearer picture of how to approach decisions, and front-line staff can be guided in customizing the value proposition for consumers.

The purpose of having good leadership is to create and regularly update the corporate vision, and direct the organization towards its realization. In order to provide unequivocal direction, the business vision needs to be clear, distinctive, memorable, motivating and meaningful, to both staff and consumers. Microsoft's original vision was very strong ('a computer on every desk and in every home'), as is Disney's ('to make people happy') and that of the International Red Cross ('to serve the most vulnerable'). The test of a strong vision is to see if people can recognize the organization from its vision statement. Many organizations either have no vision or have a vision that is weak; that is to say, it is unclear, too complex or simply irrelevant.

It has been estimated that making a business vision work is 5% creation and 95% implementation. Activating the vision starts at the top of the organization and is a process that must involve all employees. It is not until people can see the vision in terms of what it means to them that it starts to become embedded within the organization. This draws on the ability of the leader to communicate to employees the meaning of where the organization is heading and what their role in this journey will be. Marketers need to play their part by managing internal communications programmes effectively in order to support the organizational leadership and to clarify and reinforce employee understanding. Only then can vision be translated into relevant and achievable strategies.

Values

Values are a powerful and omnipresent part of organizational life. Academic researcher Milton Rokeach defines values as enduring beliefs about preferable ways of behaving, and a value system as an enduring way of organizing those beliefs (1973). In the New Consumer Marketing model corporate values support the implementation of the corporate vision. They make up the integral beliefs that guide organizational behaviour. Moreover, as their definition suggests, values are not fashion items to be changed on a regular basis; values should stand the test of time. Singapore Airlines is one company that understands this well.

Singapore Airlines
Singapore Airlines has six core values, which support its mission statement: 'We are a global company dedicated to providing air transportation services of the highest quality and earning good returns for shareholders'. Although

these words are rooted in operational and financial performance, marketing has transformed the airline into *Fortune Magazine*'s most admired airline in 2002. The key to Singapore Airline's achievement are these core values (see Table 9.1), which permeate every area of business strategy. By translating these values into actionable and measurable practices within the organization, the company is able to build value-centricity and give real substance to its brand. The airline's employees see themselves as a part of the brand and this is reflected in their work performance, adding significant value to the consumer's experience.

Table 9.1 Singapore Airlines' core values

1. Pursuit of excellence	We strive for the highest professional standards in our work and aim to be the best in everything we do.
2. Safety	We regard safety as an essential part of all our operations. We maintain and adopt practices that promote the safety of our customers and staff.
3. Customer first	Our customers are foremost in our minds all the time. We go the extra mile to exceed their expectations.
4. Concern for staff	We value our staff and care for their well-being. We treat them with respect and dignity and seek to provide them with appropriate training and development so that they can lead fulfilling careers.
5. Integrity	We strive for fairness in all our business and working relationships.
6. Teamwork	We work with pride as a worldwide team to achieve success together.

Where management action is not aligned with corporate values, the values become meaningless, as demonstrated in the fall from grace of industry giants Enron and Andersen in 2002. An organization's values are the principles that the company abides by and is willing to enforce; they are not simply the words printed on the pages of company brochures. It is all very well drawing up carefully crafted values statements and codes of practice but these become pointless if employees are permitted to contravene them. Actions speak louder than words, and an organization's values should be seen as non-negotiable, minimum standards.

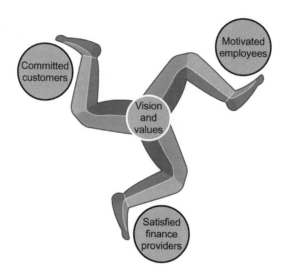

Figure 9.4 The committed enterprise. Adapted from Davidson (2002)
From the Committed Enterprise by Davidson. Reprinted by permission of Elsevier Limited

Business adviser and best-selling author Hugh Davidson pulls together the role of leadership, vision and values in his model of the 'committed enterprise' (2002). This is shown in Figure 9.4 and is based on the formula:

Committed customers + Motivated employees = Satisfied resource/finance
providers

Davidson believes that an enterprise's vision and values bind these three constituent parties (customers, employees, resource providers), by providing future direction and governing everyday decision making and behaviour. Through vision and values the needs of the three parties are aligned and they are able to move forward together. Davidson expresses this through the use of a visual symbol that dates back to Roman times, the Three Legs of Man. 'Whichever way you throw me, I stand' is the symbol's accompanying motto.

Vision and values need to be embedded in the organization and this can only be done by making them measurable and converting them into personal objectives for every member of staff. Together with leadership, they make up a complex but vital element in organizational DNA. Whether or not an organization's vision and values are realized depends on appropriate leadership and on the management of employees.

THE ROLE OF EMPLOYEES IN DEMAND SYSTEM MANAGEMENT

While marketers are confronting the shift from a production-driven to a consumption-led economy, human resource (HR) professionals are facing a similar tectonic change as employees are increasingly perceived as an organizational asset rather than a production cost. This redefinition of the role of employees is a response to the decline in manufacturing and the rise of the Information Age, which demands a radically different approach to HR management. The role of employees is a matter of concern for marketers because the impact of an organization externally is tied to what goes on internally.

The move away from manufacturing and the emergence of the knowledge worker brings in its wake a change in the asset base of the organization. As Peter Drucker says, 'the most valuable assets of a 20th-century company were its production equipment. The most valuable asset of a 21st-century institution, whether business or non-business, will be its knowledge workers and their productivity' (Drucker, 2002). This perspective forces a shift in the way in which people are evaluated within the organization. In the manufacturing economy, manual workers were regarded as a cost, which needed to be controlled and reduced, and employee management reflected this. Employee productivity was increased through investment in plant and technology. Knowledge workers, in contrast, are seen as a capital asset, whose intrinsic value can be grown. Their productivity is achieved in a very different way, by placing responsibility with the knowledge workers themselves. The emphasis in HR management today therefore tends towards self-management and autonomy. This ethos plays a crucial part in empowering staff to deliver better service, as was mentioned in Chapter 8.

The underlying assumption here is that unlike the manual workers of the production-driven era, knowledge workers own the means of production and enjoy greater levels of mobility in their careers than previous generations. This is the thesis explored in the book *Funky Business* (Nordström and Ridderstråle, 2000). The authors write, 'Karl Marx was right. The workers do control the means of production; 1.3 kilograms of brain holds the key to all our futures'. In their words, 'It's talent that makes capital dance'.

Harnessing this talent means adopting a different approach to managing people. Best-practice organizations, whose thinking has moved out of the industrial age, adopt the philosophy that they are in a more or less symbiotic relationship with employees and they create an internal value proposition to inform HR practice. The organization employs people to define, create and deliver value in the marketplace at a profit. In return for their intellectual application, development of potential and loyalty to the organization, employees receive a range of benefits.

In the same way that the external value proposition, described in Chapter 6, is made up of component factors, so too is the internal value proposition. It takes the form of a mix of two sorts of benefits and incentives. There are extrinsic ones such as pay and promotion, and intrinsic ones, which lie deep within human nature. Research shows that 'while traditional rewards and punishments can, if ill-managed, severely damage motivation, they have little beneficial effect under even the best of circumstances. It is the fuzzier things – to do with feelings of purpose, belonging, engagement – that push people to do their best' (*Harvard Business Review*, 2003).

Just as the factors that create added value for the consumer are those that are mould breaking and have never before been offered in the marketplace, the factors that create added value for employees are similarly innovative and special. These key discriminating factors set the organization apart from competitors in the eyes of employees. Occasionally, some of these differentiating factors may be 'adopted' by staff and become 'talking points', creating great word-of-mouth marketing for the organization as an employer of choice. Examples here include the free ice creams and picnic blankets made available in the summer to Microsoft's staff at their Reading facility, the three-month unpaid winter holiday, known as a 'Benidorm break', made available to older staff at Asda, and Pret A Manger's maternity package, which includes £20 towards a pair of maternity jeans and health spa vouchers upon return to work.

The internal value proposition provides the focus for the full range of HR practices. These cover recruitment, training, appraisal, promotion and succession planning, as well as redundancy and dismissal. In the 'war for talent' (Michaels et al., 2001), recruitment is critical. Best-practice organizations are looking not only for competency in prospective employees but also alignment with the organization's vision and values.

For many organizations, the most effective and efficient way to recruit the right people is to encourage existing staff to introduce new employees.

Once recruited into a best-practice organization, employees participate in the acculturation and learning processes. Whereas these two processes barely made it on to organizational agendas in the industrial age, they are now seen as key to motivating and retaining staff. Personalized and targeted learning is offered on a continuous basis, and organizations sometimes formalize this within their own learning institutions, for example, the 'universities' run by McDonald's, Disney and Unipart. Other companies are working more virtually and taking advantage of developments in IT to create learning academies on their intranets. There is also an emerging trend to provide non-work-related courses and opportunities to fulfil personal development goals. Many organizations realize the value of providing benefits related to achieving a sense of personal well-being, such as sponsoring employee memberships to sports centres and the provision of health services. Team- and company-based activities that benefit the local community or charities also characterize best-practice HR systems. Expenditure on these less-traditional HR development activities is viewed as an investment in the organization's knowledge base and is assessed accordingly. Ongoing appraisals, promotion and reward systems provide a further means of reinforcing desired internal behaviours and attitudes.

Where all of these elements of HR practice work effectively, employees will be motivated and happy to stay with the organization. This approach to HR management does not simply equate with paying them high salaries, as the winners of the 2002 '100 best companies to work for' show (McCall, 2002). Asda's experience is a good example.

Asda

Top-rated superstore Asda has annual sales of £9.7 billion and employs 117,000 people. Salaries start at £8,833. In the 1980s, the company reversed its declining fortunes by adopting a culture based on Wal-Mart's customer-friendly style. When the Asda chain was bought by the American giant Wal-Mart in 1999, the value-centric orientation in both organizations ensured a smooth transition, despite staff fears that the two cultures would clash. The underlying philosophy is that everyone must be treated as an individual and staff incentives are targeted to keep employee motivation high. For example, Asda recently introduced an employee health insurance scheme to cover male cancers. The scheme follows on from the company's 'Well Woman' cover, which has had a 50% take-up. Asda's share option scheme will see the 16,000 staff who were given shares in 1995 share an estimated £25 million when their shares schemes mature. Other loyalty incentives include a law club that provides Asda employees with legal advice for 10 pence a week, and a free investment advice service from Bradford & Bingley. These practices have helped keep the company's staff turnover down to an abnormally low figure for the sector.

Asda and other organizations that define, create and deliver a value proposition for staff that makes them an employer of choice base their strategy on a simple model that links employee satisfaction and retention with customer satisfaction and retention. Research suggests that a satisfied and stable workforce is more capable of delivering higher service quality at

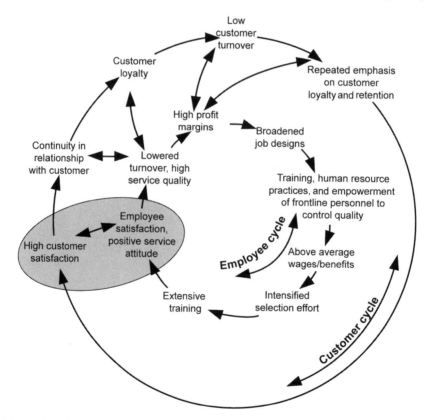

Figure 9.5 The cycle of success. Adapted from Schlesinger and Heskett (1991)
Adapted from Sloan Management Review, Vol 32, Issue 3, Spring 1991, pp. 17–28

lower cost (Schlesinger and Heskett, 1991). This leads to higher levels of customer satisfaction, which in turn impacts customer retention levels and increased profitability. This virtuous circle is shown in Figure 9.5.

THE ROLE OF KNOWLEDGE MANAGEMENT IN DEMAND SYSTEM MANAGEMENT

In today's consumption-led economy, brand owners and retailers are concentrating on becoming more productive by managing their response to consumer demand better. They are increasingly switching their business focus from cutting costs to adding value. A key means of adding value is through knowledge management processes. As a consequence, knowledge management has emerged as a major business discipline. It is driven by advances in IT and growth in the use of the Internet, which allow information to be exchanged across the world, 24 hours a day, seven days a week, all at the touch of a button. Failure to adapt knowledge management practices to this continually changing environment leads to what Arnold Kransdorff (1999/2000) has termed 'corporate amnesia', a phenomenon that prevents organizations learning from their own experiences: 'Characterized by knowledge loss, it stems from short memory, selective recall and the flexible labour market'.

In order to create differential advantage, a business needs to master the flows of information and knowledge that exist within its organization and throughout its value chain. As Lew Platt, former CEO of Hewlett-Packard, has often been quoted as saying, 'If Hewlett-Packard knew what Hewlett-Packard knows, we'd be three times as profitable'. The aim of knowledge management is to build a collective and dynamic corporate memory. The first step is to establish a process for capturing knowledge about the organization and the marketing environment.

There are two main types of knowledge: explicit knowledge and tacit knowledge. Explicit knowledge is the more tangible of the two. It represents the type of knowledge that can be captured in written or process form and easily reused. The 'what' dimension of corporate know-how is largely explicit knowledge. Tacit knowledge refers to the implicit and often ambiguous knowledge that is acquired mainly through personal experience. It is usually context-specific and provides the 'how' dimension of corporate know-how. Tacit knowledge is difficult to formalize and hard to capture. As people are generally better at talking about experiences than writing them down, new techniques to capture tacit knowledge are emerging. Based on the art of storytelling, these techniques amount to formalized oral debriefings following important organizational events. The debriefing process allows employees to create accurate records of how, why and when they performed their tasks. It requires a climate of trust, as employees need to feel that they are not relinquishing personal advantage but are adding to the greater gain, from which they too will benefit. It therefore calls for a supportive organizational culture and value system.

Knowledge itself has no intrinsic value as its value comes from being used, and, unlike other resources, knowledge grows with use. Extracting and exploiting the value of knowledge is a core competence within demand-led organizations. In managing a demand system, the knowledge management process should reflect the value-centric orientation of the organization. Knowledge about consumers and their wants and desires, competitors and internal competencies must be captured and managed to enable the superior definition, creation and delivery of the value proposition. As Professor George Day from Wharton writes, 'What distinguishes a market-driven firm is the depth and timeliness of market knowledge that enables it to anticipate market opportunities and respond faster than its rivals. When this knowledge is widely shared, it is a common reference point and assumption set that ensures the strategy is coherent rather than a disconnected set of activities' (Day, 1999).

New Consumer Marketing is concerned with generating and exploiting four kinds of knowledge. The first is knowledge about consumers, for this enables the organization to define and create a value proposition that is relevant and appealing to consumers. These subjects were covered in Chapters 6 and 7. Chapter 6 covered the generation of insight and making it actionable through segmentation, while Chapter 7 explored the process of value creation and the role of new product development, branding, positioning and pricing in achieving this.

The second kind of knowledge used in New Consumer Marketing is derived from competitor activity. Awareness and understanding of what competitors are doing and planning can help in making strategic marketing plans work. Of particular importance is an understanding of the organization's competitive position as seen from the consumer's point of view.

The third kind of knowledge, which underpins the functioning of a demand system, is process knowledge. In the New Consumer Marketing model this relates to knowledge about the three cells – value definition, value creation and value delivery. The aim is to make the core process in each cell more efficient and effective. Process knowledge comes from improved organization of the activities that support the development of insight, innovation and agility. Tacit process knowledge may well be a greater source of advantage here than explicit process knowledge.

Finally, there is the need to know about IT and how to use it smartly. Systems knowledge guides the application of IT in both externally and internally facing systems. Decisions made regarding the deployment of IT will have a fundamental impact on the success of a New Consumer Marketing approach.

Making the most of all four kinds of knowledge requires an organizational culture that recognizes the value of knowledge; enables the formulation and implementation of a strategy for knowledge management that is tied to a value-centric orientation; and creates a climate that encourages the acquisition and sharing of knowledge. Without this supporting culture, the organizational DNA is fatally flawed.

THE ROLE OF PLANNING IN DEMAND SYSTEM MANAGEMENT

Increasing turbulence in the marketplace, more demanding and sophisticated consumers, increasing environmental complexity, and the speed of technological advancement all raise questions about the wisdom of setting down in a plan the three- to five-year ambitions of an organization. How can planning be of use when times are changing so fast? Are conventional approaches agile enough to capture the dynamic complexity of the marketplace except in the very short term? In the pre-quake business environment, planning was presented as an orderly and linear sequence of steps. For many organizations it was a-once-a-year, fill-in-the-box activity. The conventional approach started with corporate and strategic planning, which covered the identification of corporate goals (including mission, vision, values, financial objectives and shareholder requirements). All of this was distilled down into a strategic marketing plan that consisted of a situational analysis, leading to a summary presented in a SWOT analysis.

Marketing objectives and strategy were then defined on the basis of this analysis, as well as factors previously noted as relevant to the organization. The fourth and final stage of marketing planning involved creating a tactical plan setting out the immediate 12 months' activity. This approach was a reflection of the make–sell model that characterized the production-driven economy.

The arrival of the New Consumer and the consumption-led economy has forced organizations to rethink their marketing planning. Business gurus such as Gary Hamel are asking questions about how useful this conventional planning exercise is when e-commerce has so dramatically foreshortened planning cycles. His 1994 book, co-authored with C. K. Prahalad, *Competing for the Future*, introduced the concept of core competencies and 'industry foresight', or the art of anticipating markets and customers five or ten years ahead. Some six years on, Hamel's later book, *Leading the Revolution* (2000), places far less emphasis on foresight because of the fast-paced nature of market development. Instead, he advises adopting 'non-linear strategies' to create entirely new business models. His focus has therefore shifted from foresight to continuous innovation. His argument is that organizations need to make the critical shift from stewardship to entrepreneurship: they should 'bring Silicon Valley inside' the organization and create internal markets for ideas, capital and talent – a philosophy borrowed from the firms at the epicentre of the dotcom revolution, where success is based on resource attraction, not resource allocation.

However, in this time of transition and in the wake of the dotcom disasters, many managers feel that ideas are not enough without sound planning. As Professor Malcolm McDonald of Cranfield School of Management explains, plans inform employees in all parts of the organization (McDonald, 1999). They are needed in order to obtain resources and support, gain commitment, and set objectives and strategy. In a demand system, planning is an important element of organizational DNA as it serves to turn the value proposition into a coherent marketing programme. The aim is to create an ongoing process approach to planning. This assists in the delivery of organizational agility. As John Coudron, CEO of Yell, the publisher of Yellow Pages, says, 'We set ourselves the target that on any Monday morning I could walk in and ask to see an updated marketing plan on a Friday. So our marketing plan was being

continually refreshed to take account of changing customer requirements'
(McDonald, 2001).

This process approach to marketing planning is explained in more detail
by Professor Nigel Piercy, also from Cranfield School of Management.
Piercy writes that planning in this way is a 'source of leverage for working
on achieving market-led strategic change, and actually making market
strategy and marketing programmes happen' (Piercy, 2002). He sees
elements such as corporate culture, management style, information flows,
organizational structures, participation and so on, treated as either
insignificant facilitating mechanisms or 'context' in conventional planning
approaches. He believes these issues are not mere context but that they are
the process, and that the way the process of planning is managed will have
a direct impact on what goes into the plan and will determine the outputs.
His advice to organizations is that they should focus on commitment and
ownership rather than techniques and formal methods, as this is what will
ultimately drive the value-centric strategy and deliver the value
proposition.

This holistic approach to managing the marketing planning process
should result in the creation of more than a physical plan. It should ensure
that plans are achievable, actionable and capable of being implemented,
that they are owned within the organization, and that they work to gain the
commitment of executives to make them happen. A major benefit of taking
a process approach to planning is that it should cease to be a once-a-year
ritual and should instead operate continuously. The planning process
should identify real information needs, and become a means of sharing
understanding of organizational strategy and challenging perceived
wisdom within the organization.

For this to happen, Piercy suggests an alternative model for managing
the planning process. This is shown in Figure 9.6. The model identifies
three process dimensions: analytical, behavioural and organizational. The
analytical dimension covers the techniques, procedures, systems and
planning models that essentially analyse and integrate data and thinking.
The process of managing planning is made more comprehensive by
including a behavioural aspect to do with how things get done. This
comprises people-related elements such as managerial perceptions,
participation levels, strategic assumptions, motivation, commitment and
ownership. The third dimension focuses on the nature of the organization,

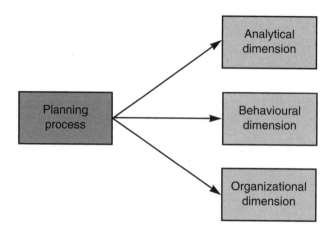

Figure 9.6 A multidimensional model of marketing planning. Adapted from Piercy (2002)

From Market-Led Strategy Change by Piercy. Reprinted by permission of Elsevier Limited

incorporating organizational structure and culture, and management signals about what actually gets priority within the organization.

Budgeting is the next step (following the creation of a plan) in making the planning process a reality. Whether a top-down/bottom-up or a bottom-up/top-down approach is taken, the budget marks the point at which the organization signals its commitment to a demand system by allocating the resources, financial and non-financial, that will make it happen. For Piercy, it is equally important that budgeting is managed as a process that also takes into account the wider analytical, behavioural and organizational dimensions discussed in relation to creating a plan.

Taking a broader approach to planning that assimilates these analytical, behavioural and organizational dimensions naturally makes the planning process more complex and less easy to manage. The danger of a poorly managed planning process is that it might result in a plan that is too focused on analysis or one that does not carry enough information, in both cases leading to a plan that is neither achievable nor actionable. Equally, vested interests may dominate the planning process, causing limited ownership and commitment on the part of other managers, and making it harder to implement. Other planning problems revolve around a lack of resources and organizational resistance to change. It is therefore important that there are agreed measures of marketing performance in place, and that the measurement results inform future strategy and practice.

THE ROLE OF MEASUREMENT IN DEMAND SYSTEM MANAGEMENT

An important aspect of New Consumer Marketing is the need to address the issue of measuring marketing performance. The model makes measurement a necessary part of the way the organization defines, creates and delivers the value proposition. As with the other six elements of organizational DNA, measurement plays a role in improving the performance of each of the three cells. Without an ongoing assessment of performance against specific criteria, the organization has no way of determining whether it is performing well; that is, whether the processes at work in the three cells are being carried out optimally. Performance results become an essential flow of information around the demand system, which serve to support the drive for insight, innovation and agility.

Marketing measurement enables marketers to become more accountable. An improvement in marketing accountability would address a key issue non-marketers have with their marketing colleagues. Many senior non-marketers perceive marketers as being 'unaccountable, untouchable, slippery and expensive', as confirmed in research using the cultural web (Baker, 2000). The research results are shown in Figure 9.7. This view gives

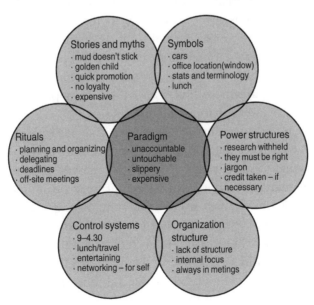

Figure 9.7 Senior non-marketers' perceptions of marketers

rise, in part, to the debate about whether and in what ways marketing contributes to a business (as first outlined in Chapter 1). Improvement in the ability of organizations to measure marketing performance would go some way towards arresting the current crisis in marketing.

Techniques to evaluate the marketing process are, at present, in an embryonic state and lack universal agreement. This is largely because the measures have not yet been developed fully, and the organizational commitment to measurement is often weak or lacking. Essentially, approaches to marketing measurement strive to find acceptable ways of measuring both 'hard' and 'soft' marketing data. Hard marketing data includes sales volume and value, market size, market share and profit margins, whereas soft marketing data is less tangible and more judgmental in nature.

However, a number of organizations are working with professional bodies to understand how performance measurement can best be accomplished. Current debate revolves around metrics that link leadership, employee satisfaction, employee retention, customer satisfaction, customer retention, sales and profitability. The emphasis on such metrics is driven by developments in customer relationship management (CRM) systems that enable organizations to measure and evaluate customer relationships as never before. For example, a growing number of accounting techniques are being used to measure customer value. These range from historic profitability analyses through lifetime value calculations, to links with shareholder value and to the computation of future value creation. The aim is to find a measurement approach that accommodates the wider interpretation of marketing.

3M(UK), referred to earlier in Chapter 7, is an example of a company that manages to balance marketing creativity without sacrificing financial control (Bowman and Gleadle, 2002). Its marketing performance is assessed by evaluating innovation in the definition, creation and delivery of the value proposition. Thirty per cent of annual company sales must be generated from products less than four years old, and 10% from products less than one year old. This distinction is refined in two further categories, with new-to-the-world developments being looked upon as 'the ideal' versus the substitution of new products for old. This represents an analysis of performance at a base level that can then be extracted down to smaller segments of customers.

As New Consumer Marketing attains 'mission-critical' status in the emerging consumption-led economy, marketing investment is gaining increasing attention from finance professionals. This trend marks part of a wider revolution in thinking about what kind of corporate assets are important in today's business environment. Intangible business assets, such as knowledge about consumers and markets, and corporate know-how about defining, creating and delivering the value proposition, are assuming new importance. The race is now on to find robust methods of evaluating and quantifying such assets for the benefit of corporate management and the wider investment community.

SUMMARY POINTS

- Demand system management is about managing a 'living' system of cells that house the key processes which drive insight, innovation and agility and enable the organization to be responsive to the complex demands of the New Consumer.

- There are seven elements of organizational DNA, which make a demand system viable. Each enables the three cells to optimize performance, thus ensuring competitive survival.

- Intuition is the spark that enables employees to base decisions on an understanding of consumers' behaviour, thoughts and feelings.

- Culture surfaces in everyday organizational life as knowledge about the 'way things are done around here'.

- Leadership is about demonstrating an ability to engage others in achieving the organization's mission, communicating the corporate vision, and upholding the corporate values.

- Corporate vision answers the question 'where are we going?', while corporate values are embedded standards and behaviours that provide guidance on how to get there. Corporate vision has to be created and refreshed whereas corporate values endure.

- Employees today are valued as a capital asset and are wooed by an internal value proposition that informs all aspects of HR practice.

- Knowledge management is about building an organizational memory, made up of explicit and tacit knowledge. It requires an organizational climate of trust.

- Planning is an ongoing process that encompasses analytical, behavioural and organizational aspects, which extend beyond the physical marketing plan.

- Measurement enables marketers to become accountable and provides knowledge about the effectiveness and efficacy of the demand system.

CONCLUDING REMARKS

Establishing the case for New Consumer Marketing as a business discipline and presenting a framework for its conceptualization has been the main aim of this book. The fundamental argument for advancing New Consumer Marketing is that a value-centric orientation needs to replace the retention orientation that has dominated marketing practice for the past decade or so. The shift in the macro-marketing environment from a production-driven to a consumption-led economy means taking the consumer as the point of departure for the organization, and not its final destination. In this dynamically complex new marketplace, marketing practice needs to be viewed as systemic and holistic. By offering such an approach to managing the definition, creation and delivery of value, the New Consumer Marketing model aims to assist managers in developing and implementing successful consumer marketing strategies. There remains, however, considerable scope for debate and for further research in this important area.

Feedback from readers is welcomed and should be directed to s.l.baker@cranfield.ac.uk.

Notes

Chapter 1

[1] Discussion of CRM in this chapter is informed by the work of the Cranfield CRM Research Forum directed by Dr Moira Clark. Visit www.cranfield-crm.org.

[2] Statistics used in this section are drawn from: EIU Viewswire (2002); www.skillbase.dfee.gov.uk; www.hesa.ac.uk; and Nellis and Figuera (2002).

Chapter 2

[1] For more on the history and sociology of consumption, see Corrigan (1997).

[2] For the background to consumerism, see John (1994). For more on today's consumer rights agenda, visit www.which.co.uk.

[3] For more on the post-modern condition refer to the following academic authors: Stephen Brown (author of the very readable *Postmodern Marketing*), Jean Baurillard, Bernard Cova and Maurice Holbrook.

Chapter 3

[1] The Cap Gemini Ernst & Young research referred to in the chapter was carried out for the Insight Programme (directed by Andre Klimczak). Visit www.cgey.com.

[2] The Verdict research was reported at the Marketing Society's Retail Forum, April 2002 and in Hyman (2002). Other references for this chapter rely on data and analysis carried in Verdict publications. Visit www.verdict.co.uk. See also Seth and Randall (2001), which contains useful analysis of trends in international grocery retailing.

Chapter 4

[1] For more on a post-modern approach to consumer behaviour, see the following academic authors: Stephen Brown, Jean Baurillard, Bernard Cova and Maurice Holbrook.

[2] Treacy and Wiersema (1995), Doyle (2000), Capon and Hulbert (2001) and Piercy (2002) highlight value as the new key driver of strategy in marketing.

Chapter 5

[1] Womack et al. (1990) describe the concept of leanness. See also references in Chapter 8.

Chapter 6

[1] For an overview of means–end theory, see Baker (2002). The key academic paper to refer to is Gutman (1982).

[2] For an overview of grounded theory, see Glaser and Strauss (1967).

[3] Discussion here and elsewhere in this chapter draws on Baker and Mouncey (2002).

Chapter 7

[1] The Dell case study referred to in this book is based on the following sources: (Hall, 2002; Dell and Fredman, 1999; Dell, 2002).

[2] Background reference paper: Bowman and Gleadle (2002).

[3] Taken from the Annual Marketing Society Lecture given by Niall FitzGerald, Chairman of Unilever, in London on 19 June 2001.

[4] Taken from the author's PhD research. For an overview of means–end theory, see Baker (2002).

Chapter 8

[1] The agile supply chain is a concept that has been developed at Cranfield School of Management within the Cranfield Centre for Logistics and Supply Chain Management. This definition of agility comes from Christopher and Towill (2000). See also the work of Professor Alan Harrison, including Harrison and Hoek (2002).

[2] Service blueprinting is associated with the work of Lynn Shostack. See Shostack (1987).

[3] The philosophy and implementation of leanness as a management concept was set out in Womack et al. (1990).

[4] Key Account Management is a concept that has been developed at Cranfield School of Management and is most closely associated with Professor Malcolm McDonald. See McDonald et al. (2002).

Chapter 9

[1] This definition of Theory of Mind is taken from 'Psychology of autism', a presentation made by Professor Uta Frith at the National Autistic Society's 40th Anniversary International Conference, London, September 2002. See also the references to Theory of Mind made by Professor Jean Aitchison in the 1996 BBC Reith Lectures, published as *The Language Web* by Cambridge University Press, 1996.

[2] See Bennis and Thomas (2002) for an overview on what makes a great leader.

References

Allford, R., Evans, N. and Ward, C. (2002) A step forward in understanding shoppers using segmentation techniques, presented at the ESOMAR Conference: Consolidation or Renewal?, Barcelona, September.

Baker, S. (2000) What non-marketers think about you, *Marketing Business*, supplement on Better Marketing Measurement, September.

Baker, S. (2002) Laddering: making sense of meaning, in Partington, D. (ed.) *Essential Skills for Management Research*. Sage: London, ch. 12.

Baker, S. and Mouncey, P. (2002) New Consumer Marketing: The implications for market research, presented at the ESOMAR Conference: Consolidation or Renewal?, Barcelona, September.

Bennis, W. and Thomas, R. (2002) Crucibles of leadership, *Harvard Business Review*, 80(9), 39–45, September.

Berners-Lee, T. and Fischetti, M. (1999) *Weaving the Web: the Original Design and Ultimate Destiny of the World Wide Web By Its Inventor*. HarperSanFrancisco: San Francisco, CA.

Booz, Allen & Hamilton (1982) *New Product Management for the 1980s*. Booz, Allen & Hamilton: New York.

Bowman, C. and Gleadle, P. (2002) Culture as a dynamic capability: the case of 3M in the UK, US Academy of Management conference paper, presented at AOM2002, Denver, Colorado.

Brown, J.S. and Duguid, P. (2000) *The Social Life of Information*. Harvard Business School Press: Boston, MA.

Brown, S. (1995) *Postmodern Marketing*. Routledge: London.

Capon, N. and Hulbert, J.M. (2001) *Marketing Management in the 21st Century*. Prentice Hall: Upper Saddle River, NJ.

Chartered Institute of Marketing (1994) *Marketing – The Challenge of Change, A Major Study into the Future of Marketing in Key British Enterprises*. Chartered Institute of Marketing: London.

Child, P. (2002) Taking Tesco global, *The McKinsey Quarterly*, 3.

Christopher, M. (1992) *The Customer Service Planner*. Butterworth-Heinemann: Oxford.

Christopher, M. (1998) *Logistics and Supply Chain Management*, 2nd edn. FT Prentice Hall: Harlow.

Christopher, M. (2001) Breaking down the boundaries: the supply chain management process, in M. McDonald, M. Christopher, S. Knox and A. Payne (eds) *Creating a Company for Customers*. FT Prentice Hall: Harlow.

Christopher, M. and Peck, H. (1997) *Marketing Logistics*. Butterworth-Heinemann: Oxford.

Christopher, M. and Towill, D. (2000) *Don't lean too far - distinguishing between the lean and agile manufacturing paradigms*, Proceedings MIM Conference, Aston (ISSN 1359-8546).

Christopher, M., Payne, A. and Ballantyne, D. (1991) *Relationship Marketing: Bringing Quality, Customer Service and Marketing Together*. Butterworth-Heinemann: Oxford.

Christopher, M., Payne, A. and Ballantyne, D. (2002) *Relationship Marketing: Creating Stakeholder Value*. Butterworth-Heinemann: Oxford.

Clark, M. (1999) The recruitment and internal marketing domains, in H. Peck, A. Payne, M. Christopher and M. Clark (eds), *Relationship Marketing Strategy and Implementation*. Butterworth-Heinemann: Oxford.

Cooper, R. (1993) *Winning at New Products: Accelerating the Process from Idea to Launch*. Addison-Wesley: Reading, MA.

Corrigan, P. (1997) *The Sociology of Consumption*. Sage: London.

Cross, R. and Prusak, L. (2002) The people who make organisations go – or stop, *Harvard Business Review*, 80(6), 104–112, June.

Davidson, H. (2002) *The Committed Enterprise*. Butterworth-Heinemann: Oxford.

Day, G. (1999) *The Market Driven Organisation*. Free Press: New York.

Dell, M. (2002) Inspiring innovation, *Harvard Business Review*, 80(8), 41, August.

Dell, M. and Fredman, C. (1999) *Direct from Dell, Strategies that Revolutionized an Industry*. HarperBusiness: New York.

Doyle, P. (2000) *Value Based Marketing – Marketing Strategies for Corporate Growth and Shareholder Value*. John Wiley & Sons: Chichester.

Drucker, P. (1985) *Innovation and Entrepreneurship: Practice and Principles*. Harper & Row: New York.

Drucker, P. (2002) *Management Challenges for the 21st Century*. Butterworth-Heinemann: Oxford.

Dyck, W. van (2002) *Managing Complexity in Radical Innovation Projects: The Need for Paradigm Shifts?* Paper presented at Cranfield School of Management.

EIU Viewswire (2002) *The Decline of Manufacturing*, 8 March.

Evans, M. (2001) Decoding competitive propositions: a semiotic alternative to traditional advertising research, presented at the MRS Conference, 169–181.

Fournier, S. (1996) Understanding consumer–brand relationships, Harvard Business School working paper 98-018.

Gates, B. and Hemingway, C. (1999) *Business @ the Speed of Thought*. Warner Books: New York.

Gattorna, J. (ed.) (1998) *Strategic Supply Chain Alignment*. Gower: Aldershot.

Geus, A. de (1999) *The Living Company: Growth, Learning and Longevity in Business*, Nicholas Brealey: London.

Glaser, B.G. and Strauss, A.L. (1967) *The Discovery of Grounded Theory: Strategies for Qualitative Research*. Aldine: Chicago, IL.

Gleick, J. (1987) *Chaos: Making a New Science*. Viking: New York.

Godin, S. (1999) *Permission Marketing: Turning Strangers into Friends, and Friends into Customers*. Simon & Schuster: New York.

Goldman, S., Nagel, R. and Preiss, K. (1995) *Agile Competitors and Virtual Organizations: Strategies for Enriching the Customer*. Van Nostrand Reinhold: New York.

Gordon, W. (1999) *Goodthinking – A Guide to Qualitative Research*. Admap: Henley on Thames.

Gordon, W. (2001) The dark room of the mind – what does neuro-psychology now tell us about brands?, presented at AQR/QRCA Conference – Qualitative Research in the 21st Century, Paris, 18–20 April.

Grant, J. (1999) *The New Marketing Manifesto*, Texere: London.

Gutman, J. (1982) A means–end chain model based on consumer categorization processes, *Journal of Marketing*, 46(2), 60–62.

Hall, A. (2002) The boy who lived the American dream, *The Sunday Times*, 1 December.

Hamel, G. (2000) *Leading the Revolution*. Harvard Business School Press: Boston, MA.

Hamel, G. and Prahalad, C.K. (1994) *Competing for the Future*. Harvard Business School Press: Boston, MA.

Hanby, T. (1999) Brands – dead or alive?, *Journal of the Market Research Society*, 41(1), 7–18.

Handy, C. (1989) *The Age of Unreason*. Harvard Business School Press: Boston, MA.

Handy, C. (1994) *The Empty Raincoat: Making Sense of the Future*. Hutchinson: London.

Handy, C. (1997) *The Hungry Spirit: Beyond Capitalism – A Quest for Purpose in the Modern World*. Hutchinson: London.

Harrison, A. and Hoek, R.I. van (2002) *Logistics Management and Strategy*. FT Prentice Hall: Harlow.

Harvard Business Review (2003) *The Best of HBR on Motivation,* 81(1), 8, January.

Hertz, N. (2001) *Silent Takeover: Global Capitalism and the Death of Democracy*. Free Press: New York.

Hyman, R. (2002) The retail roller-coaster: message from the high street, *Market Leader*, (17), 46–50.

John, R. (ed.) (1994) *The Consumer Revolution, Redressing the Balance*. Hodder & Stoughton: London.

Johnson, G. and Scholes, K. (1992) *Exploring Corporate Strategy*. Prentice Hall: London.

Kim, W.C. and Mauborgne, R. (1997) Value innovation: the strategic logic of high growth, *Harvard Business Review*, 75(1), 102–112, January/February.

Kim, W.C. and Mauborgne, R. (1999a) Creating new market space, *Harvard Business Review*, 77(1), 83–93, January/February.

Kim, W.C. and Mauborgne, R. (1999b) Strategy, value innovation and the knowledge economy, *Sloan Management Review*, 40(3), 41–54.

Kim, W.C. and Mauborgne, R. (2000) Knowing a winning business idea when you see one, *Harvard Business Review*, 78(5), 129–141, September/October.

Klein, N. (2000) *No Logo: Taking Aim at the Brand Bullies*. Picador: New York.

Kransdorff, A. (1999/2000) The other 'virus' that is bugging industry, *Market Leader*, (7), 27–29, Winter.

Lannon, J. and Cooper, P. (1983) Humanistic advertising: a holistic cultural perspective, *International Journal of Advertising*, 2(3), 195–213.

Lauterborn, R. (1991) From 4Ps to 4Cs, *Advertising Age*, 61(41), 26, 1 October.

McCall, A. (ed.) (2002) *The Sunday Times 100 Best Companies to Work For. The Sunday Times*, 24 March.

McCracken, G.D. (1988) *Culture and Consumption: New Approaches to the Symbolic Character of Consumer Goods and Activities*. Indiana University Press: Bloomington, IN.

McDonald, M. (1999) *Marketing Plans, How To Prepare Them, How To Use Them.* Butterworth-Heinemann: Oxford.

McDonald, M. (2001) Getting back to basics: the market understanding process, in M. McDonald, M. Christopher, S. Knox and A. Payne (eds) *Creating a Company for Customers.* FT Prentice Hall: Harlow, ch. 2.

McDonald, M., Rogers, B. and Woodburn, D. (2002) *Key Customers: How To Manage them Profitably.* Butterworth-Heinemann: Oxford.

McGregor, D. (1960) *The Human Side of Enterprise.* McGraw-Hill: New York.

Michaels, E., Handfield-Jones, H. and Axelrod, B. (2001) *The War for Talent.* Harvard Business School Press: Boston, MA.

Mitchell, A. (2001) *Right Side Up: Building Brands in the Age of the Organized Consumer.* HarperCollinsBusiness: London.

Moir, L. (2001) Why managers and organisations must embrace CSR, *Management Focus*, Cranfield School of Management, (17)13, Winter.

Negroponte, N. (1995) *Being Digital.* Knopf: New York.

Nellis, J. and Figueira, C. (2002) Is there a future for UK Manufacturing?, *Management Focus*, Cranfield School of Management, (19) 19–21, Winter.

Nordström, K. and Ridderstråle, J. (2000) *Funky Business: Talent Makes Capital Dance.* ft.com: Harlow.

Pascale, R.T. (1990) *Managing on the Edge: How the Smartest Companies Use Conflict to Stay Ahead.* Viking: New York.

Pascale, R.T., Millemann, M. and Gioja, L. (2000) *Surfing the Edge of Chaos: The Laws of Nature and the New Laws of Business.* Crown Business: New York.

Piercy, N. (2002) *Market-Led Strategic Change: A Guide to Transforming the Process of Going to Market*, 3rd edn. Butterworth-Heinemann: Oxford.

Pine, B.J. and Gilmore, J.H. (1998) Welcome to the experience economy, *Harvard Business Review*, 76(4), 97–105, July/August.

Pine, B.J. and Gilmore, J.H. (1999) *The Experience Economy: Work is Theatre and Every Business a Stage.* Harvard Business School Press: Boston, MA.

PricewaterhouseCoopers (1999) *Global Growth and Innovation*, survey. PricewaterhouseCoopers: London.

Reichheld, F.F. and Teal, T. (1996) *The Loyalty Effect: The Hidden Force Behind Growth, Profits, and Lasting Value.* Harvard Business School Press: Boston, MA.

Rokeach, M. (1973) *The Nature of Human Values.* Free Press: New York.

Sawhney, M. and Kotler, P. (2001) Marketing in the age of information democracy, in a chapter in D. Iacobucci (ed.) *Kellogg on Marketing.* John Wiley & Sons: Chichester.

Schlesinger, L.A. and Heskett, J.L. (1991) Breaking the cycle of failure in services, *Sloan Management Review*, Spring, 17–28.

Schultz, D.E. and Lindberg-Repo, K. (2002) Building holistic relationship communication programs in an interactive marketplace, presented at the ESOMAR Conference, Consolidation or Renewal?, Barcelona, September 2002.

Seth, A. and Randall, G. (2001) *The Grocers: The Rise and Rise of the Supermarket Chains*. London: Kogan Page.

Seybold, P., Lewis, J.M. and Marshak, R.T. (2001) *The Customer Revolution: How to Thrive When Customers Are in Control*. Random House: New York.

Shostack, L. (1987) Service positioning through structural change, *Journal of Marketing*, (51), 34–43, January.

Smith, D. and Fletcher, J. (2001) *Inside Information*. John Wiley & Sons: Chichester.

Tapscott, D. (1996) *The Digital Economy: Promise and Peril in the Age of Networked Intelligence*. McGraw-Hill: New York.

Tapscott, D. (1998) *Growing Up Digital: The Rise of the Net Generation*. McGraw-Hill: New York.

Tapscott, D., Lowy, A. and Ticoll, D. (2000) *Digital Capital: Harnessing the Power of Business Webs*. Harvard Business School Press: Boston, MA.

Taylor, F.W. (1967) *Principles of Scientific Management*. W.W. Norton: New York (first published 1911).

Toffler, A. (1970) *Future Shock*. Random House: New York (out of print).

Treacy, M. and Wiersema, F.D. (1995) *The Discipline of Market Leaders: Choose Your Customers, Narrow Your Focus, Dominate Your Market*. Addison-Wesley: Reading, MA.

Womack, J.P., Jones, D.T. and Roos, D. (1990) *The Machine that Changed the World*. Rawson Associates: New York.

Index